GIVING UP THE GAME

by Eric Durham

Printed in the United States of America

ISBN: 978-0-692-36732-2

POET SOUL   Poet Soul Entertainment
ENTERTAINMENT

To my wife, Nikki,

You are my beautiful queen and I am eternally

grateful for your unwavering love and support.

To my precious daughters,

Erica, Rachel, and Faith,

I am more than a proud father. I am humbled

that God saw me fit to place you all in my life.

May you continue to blossom into the best you

He has created you to be.

CONTENTS

CONTENTS

INTRODUCTION

Before meeting my wife, I thought I was some kind of player or mack-daddy. My homeboys and I would brag to one another about how quick we scored with some new lady we met at the club, grocery store, laundromat, etc. Life during my 20's was a continual chase to find myself in the good graces of all of the young women I met. I have had several flings, one-night stands and even long-lasting relationships. I was never satisfied until I met a young lady who made me turn in my player card.

My wife is my best friend. I know that there was truly nothing I did to deserve such a wonderful woman. When I think of my wife, I think to myself, "This is what faithfulness and commitment looks like." My wife has been with me and stuck by me through all manner of struggles, successes and failings. At the end of the day, even when she can't stand me sometimes, she stills keeps her commitment to God and to our marriage vows. Some people marry because they've fallen in love with the mere idea of marriage. But when the road gets rough, they pack up and run. I recall older men saying how they have grown to love their wives more over the years. I couldn't understand that because the way I felt about Nikki when we first started dating, I truly thought that I couldn't love anyone more than I loved her. I thought that I was at the peak of Love's Mountain and couldn't get any higher. I understand that ol' saying now. I, too, have grown more in love with my wife over the years. I admire her because she's dedicated, works hard, is great mother and wife, educated, and most importantly, loves God. She's not perfect. None of us are. However, God gave me exactly what I prayed for.

My wife tells me that I'm her best friend and if she had to do it again, she would. But it wasn't always this way. After we got married, our personalities started to clash – a lot. We got along well enough, but I was used to good-looking "fast" women. Nikki was good-looking, but "slow" if you know what I mean – not the short bus "slow" either. I wasn't used to having to warm up the oven because it was fairly easy to get what I wanted as a single man in a world where everyone seemed to be hot and ready to go. I started thinking that she wasn't pleased with me sexually, but then my pride would kick in. During arguments, I would say stupid things like, "This woman and that woman loved how I put it on them. Some of them still want me to this very day!" Of all of the bonehead things I could do, I would say the very thing to shut her down emotionally. When the arguments would calm down, she would explain that not desiring me sexually wasn't the issue. She has the type of personality where she allows stress to take up a lot of space in her mind. Things like the business of life, our children, and other things would get in the way, affecting her to the point where she was just too stressed to even think about sex. This was only area we struggled in. But I'm here to testify that if you hang in there long enough, pray, and try to reach out to your partner in love to see life through their eyes, things will change for you as it did for us.

As time passed and we grew older, we started calmly talking about our relationship without running from serious issues that needed to be discussed. We had gotten to the place where we could agree to disagree without it being World War III.

As I see it, the problem regarding relationships is that most people try to wing it. People would never think of buying a car without an owner's manual or driving without first knowing the rules of the road. People don't usually get behind the wheel of a car without first taking driving lessons or learning from an experienced instructor. However, people seem to be notorious at overestimating their abilities when it comes to relationships. Two of the most impactful things in a person's life is marriage and raising children.

There are many that rush into a relationship or into starting a family when sadly, they don't even take the time to get to know themselves.

Life doesn't come with an owner's manual, folks. There are a lot of good books and classes out there that would greatly assist you in these aforementioned areas of marriage and child-rearing. One of the best books in my opinion is the Bible. Truth be told, most gurus, counselors and bestselling authors take from the Bible. They reword it to omit the religious context, then repackage it to sell to the public as an original idea - and make millions off of it. I know this for a fact because I have a large library at home with a lot of inspirational, self-help, and business books. I come across so many quotes that are straight from the Bible, many only slightly tweaked. All I can do is laugh and say to myself that I could have saved myself a lot of my money by sticking with the original material. I don't knock them, though. Many times they do put a fresh perspective on certain topics.

A loving relationship can bring you to the height of ecstasy, but one with the wrong person can leave you bleeding and scarred on the battlefield of love. If you want to be successful in the area of relationships – romantic, platonic, business, or otherwise, then this book is for you.

I've learned a lot over the years and wrote this book in hopes that it would be a catalyst for change in the lives of those who want and need it. I want people to recognize game in others as well as weakness in themselves that causes us to accept certain things and people into our lives.

My aim is to be transparent because this is what young women and men need in order to help them know what to look out for as well as avoid so that they don't make the same mistakes many have made before them – mistakes made simply from ignorance.

Enjoy!

GIVING UP THE GAME

GIVING UP THE GAME

CHAPTER ONE

LOST IN EMOTION

My childhood friends, Jeff and Ron, used to call me a sucker for love. I would have to agree with them although I hated when they would say it to me. Growing up, I always wanted someone to love me for me - to see me, to look past the silly jokester, thug, or whoever I was trying to be in that moment of time. I wondered if I'd ever find true love. I would see so many couples holding hands with that look in their eyes as though time and space didn't matter when they were in each other's embrace. To me, a relationship signified that I had arrived - that I was a man.

It wasn't until high school that I started to realize that I didn't look half bad, but I was so nervous when it came to trying to talk to a young lady who peaked my interest. I was usually at a loss for words and came across like a corn ball many times. For some reason, my confidence skyrocketed after high school. I would hook up with women without much effort at all. It didn't matter whether they were fat, skinny, tall, short, good-looking, not so good-looking, any complexion. It was all good. The problem was that because of my personal idiosyncrasies and wrong

1

belief systems, I would use their approval in order to validate my self-worth. The cool dudes I hung out with showed themselves as aloof. They behaved as though nothing affected them. This characteristic seemed to have made women curious and wanting to be all up in their space. Getting love from the honeys became addictive.

Temporarily, I grew weary of all of the heart aches that came along with the break-ups. During the down time, I would spend time alone at home listening to slow songs and reminiscing. It wasn't long before I was back in the clubs looking for another hottie.

In the early 90's, rap music started to become very misogynistic. Rappers basically called brothers stupid for falling in love. They touted that women were no good as if they were genetically predisposed to cheating. Being influenced by this music, men everywhere started to have a pimp or "mack" mentality. As I started taking on this mentality myself, it seemed as if I became more interesting to females of all caliber. I felt freer to be myself around the ladies because of this. In reality, I wasn't being myself because I refused to give my heart to anyone even though it was what I inwardly really desired.

Nevertheless, I started to enjoy the fun and freedom I felt with this new mindset spawned by the music which amplified the unfaithfulness of women (not that I was any better). I've fooled around with women who were engaged, married, and who had boyfriends. Seeing how easy it was to hook up with women, validated their disloyalty. It pushed me further into a shell of coldness as I became more convinced that I would be stupid to give myself fully to any woman.

Leading with the heart was too dangerous of a proposition for me to consider at that time because I had "proof" that women couldn't be trusted as far as I could spit. As it seemed like everyone was "cutting a corner," I nestled into playing the game. I'm not going to lie. Taking on the new mentality actually caused me more pain in the long run. Growing up, I thought that life was supposed to be a certain way. I later discovered that I needed to get out of the fantasy land if I didn't want to get hurt and be played like a fool. After all, if the rappers said it, it must have been true right?

The major problem was that I didn't fully understand what love really was at the time. Love is commitment. It is action. Yes, emotion is involved, however, I learned that if I allowed my emotions to lead me, I would always find myself in and out of other people's beds looking for the next emotional high. That roller coaster was one scary ride. On one hand, I would experience intense feelings for a woman with a desire to sleep with her, let go and truly fall in love. On the other hand, I'd attempt to immediately shut off any romantic feelings for that woman so I didn't get caught up.

I tried to give the love thing a chance when I got into a relationship where I had my first child. This relationship was so crazy and chaotic that anyone would be surprised that either one of us is still alive! What we went through was totally wild to say the least.

Now, here's the moment where I put in a shameless plug. Smile. If you would like to read more about that story, you can purchase my book "Transformed: The Past Doesn't Have To Define Your Future" which is available on Amazon.com.

Anyway, we both thought the other was crazy. I eventually ended that three-year relationship and moved back home to Tampa, FL.

After that break-up, I tried to put my wild ways behind me. I started going to church as a result of an invitation from an old friend. I was hurt and tried to heal, but I was attempting to do it in a vacuum - staying to myself, just going to work and coming back home. A few months later, my child's mother called me and put the mac game down on me. Can you believe the nerve of her? You guessed it. I fell for it. I believed her when she said she had changed. Blah, blah, blah. She moved back to Tampa, but I didn't let her move in with me so I could reduce the temptation of us becoming sexually intimate again. I was really trying to do the right thing by God.

Long story short, she started running around on me with other guys. I ended up catching her at the hotel with someone. A week or so later, I would play the forgiving role and ask her to come back to me so we could work things out. After all, we had a child together. I certainly wasn't a saint myself, though. I got so focused on her that I totally forgot about my new relationship with God. Being lost in emotion, I allowed myself to get sucked back into my old lifestyle of debauchery.

So there I was, single again. It was time to catch up with the homeboys and run the streets to make up for lost time. I returned to doing to women what I didn't want them to do to me which was to hurt them and leave scars. I started getting beside myself and thought that my stuff didn't stink. I started to get my shine on when I bought my first BMW, dressed every day like a real player should, and draped myself in gold. It was 1995 and I was 25, reeking of pride. My partners and I would be in just about every club almost every day of the week. I sought to be the life of the party by buying drinks for everyone. I went from dancing and having fun when I was a bit younger to holding up the wall, looking serious and sipping on Cognac with my partner waiting for women to approach so I could put my game down.

I was hustling at the time so this afforded me the ability to live an imaginary Hollywood lifestyle (by the way only lasted a short period of time before everything fell apart). Eventually, in 1996, a few events began to change my perspective on being a player.

I rented an apartment close to the University of South Florida (USF). My friends and I used to have fun going to fraternity and sorority parties. Some of the girls would sneak us into their dorms after curfew. They were away from mom and dad and for a lot of them, this was their first taste of freedom. They had the good-girl image by day, but by night and a few drinks later, they became totally different people.

I started to miss being in a committed relationship, you know, having someone to come home to at night. I guess you could say that "the sucker for love" had returned. I got involved with a beautiful dark-skinned woman at USF and we messed around for a while. The only problem was that it was just a sex thing for her. There were many times when I simply wanted her to stay around longer to talk and chill. She was young and only looking for fun so I had to reluctantly accept that. I just couldn't shake the feeling that I was being used.

Feeling used didn't stop me, though. I went from one fling to another. I recall this fine little lady who was in the police academy. I told my neighbor to hook me up with her. My female neighbor was overweight. I'd gotten out of my big-girl phase so I never tried to get with her. But she said in order for her to hook me up with her friend, I would have to sleep with her. So they both came over and all three of us we were all in the bedroom together. In another instance, a female who came over looking for my friend ended up giving me the goods because he wasn't around. I began to feel like it was starting to be too easy for me to get laid. Yet another night shortly after that incident, I met a girl from the club and she came home with me that same night. We woke up the morning after a night of sex and didn't even know each other's name which was embarrassing to say the least. Ok. I'll stop there. Sex was sport to me because I didn't know the real purpose for it at the time. Sex was originally designed to glorify God (in marriage), bring forth children, express intimacy, provide comfort, and bless the spouse. The really weird thing is that the more experienced a man is, this seems to turn women on. On the other hand, if a woman has had several sexual partners before marriage, we men want to call them whores. Come on fellas, you know it's true.

One of the last flings I had that year totally shook me up emotionally. I mean, I was messed up. Wait, this one needs a little background so bear with me. This particular young lady was the ex-girlfriend of the guy my child's mother became involved with. The guy was real cool with me and I liked him. I don't think he knew I was messing with his ex-girlfriend, but he knew I was aware of his relationship with my ex. I actually didn't know my new boo had recently broken up with my guy friend until after we got involved.

Anyway, she would come over like three times a week for sex only. She was cool and we would have small talk and joke here and there, but after a while, I started really liking this girl and wanted to take the relationship to another level. One day, when she came over, instead of doing our regular routine, I wanted to get personal and talk about her life and share my thoughts with her. I was told in no uncertain terms that if I wasn't going to have sex with her, she was going to leave. I paused for a minute – shocked. Then I responded like Martin Lawrence, "Oh, naw girl, you know how I do. I'm about to tear that up!" I reality, I was the one that was tore up on the inside. I felt like a trick, like a whore. I felt used.

This experience was finally the turning point for me. I really started to understand how women felt when men would treat them as objects. It was like a veil was taken off of my eyes. This game didn't feel fun anymore. I felt stupid for participating in it - for thinking that the game provided me some type of freedom. Ultimately, the game left me torn, emotionally cold, and confused.

The problem wasn't that women were whores as the rappers and dudes on the block used to tell me. The problem was the person I had become and the type of women I chose. The problem was my own flawed perspective that so many young men still hold today. I would like to say that I immediately changed after this event, but that wasn't the case. It would take me a few more years of focused self-development and commitment to change while on the journey to becoming the best version of myself. Am I this great, wise man today - a man who doesn't fail? The answer to that question would be no, however, I strive every day to do right and be honorable. I strive to correct my mistakes when I do make them and am quick to apologize when I hurt or offend anyone, especially my wife.

GIVING UP THE GAME

Today, I am a better man because of my wife's love and her commitment to an imperfect man. I have to say that I experience the love and faithfulness of God through her. She is all that I need in a mate. I'm learning to love her better every day. Through all of our ups, downs, and misunderstandings, we have not thrown in the towel. We refused to be quitters. Not only are our kids dependent on us, but society at large needs to see that there is substance to this thing called marriage. Marriage can work and be fulfilling. Marriage is the building block and stabilizing factor for a society. Broken homes and marriages are what contribute to the breakdown of societies. There's no surprise that as divorce rates are on the rise, our nation is going downhill... fast.

<u>NOTES</u>

<u>NOTES</u>

CHAPTER TWO

WELCOME TO THE GAME

In any game, a person participates with the ultimate goal in mind - to win. Period. In the arena of love and intimate relationships, games can range from innocent tests to gauge the person's interest, attraction, or commitment level to the most despicable, self-centered forms of control and manipulation via devious methods. You cannot respond to a game appropriately until you first recognize you're in one. Many stay stuck in a game because no one will outright tell you, "Hey dummy, I'm running a game on you!" It's left up to you to figure out. Anyone can get caught up in a game, even the most experienced player. Some, having recognized that they're in a game, decide to play it anyway because of some perceived advantage they feel they can gain from the relationship. Some, having found themselves in a game, look at it as a challenge and want to see if they can conquer the gamer and the game or perhaps "change" the gamer in hopes to be that person's savior/lover. For some, they are totally repulsed by the notion that someone would have the nerve to be anything other than "straight up" that they abruptly end the relationship because they value themselves and their time too much for what they consider foolishness and disrespect.

Understand this. In the first three to six months of any new relationship, who you are seeing is "the representative." People will always put their best foot forward when meeting someone new. This is also a time when it really is not advisable to commit to someone because you are most likely running on oxytocin. What is oxytocin? Oxytocin is a chemical that creates a sense of well-being and euphoria that comes with falling madly in love. Some have called this period one of temporary insanity because the brain is hijacked by those chemicals, interfering with the ability to think clearly. This is also a time when, if you're not careful, you'll look back on it and ask yourself why in the world you did something so stupid. If you are among the one percent who have always kept it real, well congratulations. But for the rest of us who have run game at some point in our lives, even if innocently, this chapter is for you.

Mankind's ability to deceive itself and others is great and people are deceived when they are not able to discern twisted information or outright lies. The game is cold, folks. The old saying says not to hate the player, but hate the game. I tell you honestly, I don't really care for players that much either. I don't like the politicians that play the people. I don't like those in the media industry who spin the news in such a way that the audience doesn't really get the whole story and as a result, leads them to draw inaccurate conclusions. I can go on my rant, but I'll stop here before I go down a rabbit trail.

Why the game? Why can't people just be straight up? Just look around you. We are raised in a way, especially in western civilization, that in order to get on top, we have to do it at the expense of others because there is just simply not enough for everyone to "have." In other cultures, there is a strong sense of togetherness - people operating as one unit. If one suffers, all suffers. If one succeeds, all succeed. That's not always the case here in the United States, at least not from my perspective and what history suggests. You may choose to disagree. From video games to Wall Street, we have this aggressive desire to dominate, to subjugate and control people and systems for our own self-interests. There remains an, "I've got mine. You'd better get yours," dog-eat-dog mentality. This is opposed to the, "This is how I did it and I'll help you by giving you a hand up," my brother's keeper mentality.

So as long as a culture exists that caters to a rugged independent "John Wayne" mentality where acquiring more things and status are more important than people, the game will always be in play. People play the game because of distrust. Who can find a totally trustworthy person these days anyway? People are hedging their bets trying to insulate themselves from hurt. In this regard, it makes sense play the game. The one who can get through the game of love with the fewest scars is the winner, right?

This reminds me of the futuristic science fiction movie entitled *The Matrix*. This movie poses that everyone is born into a system where nothing is as it seems and the system is actually feeding off of its subjects, the energy unit. I think that there are some truths we can pull from this movie. Anyone who has studied sociology learns that we are born into systems that exert a great amount of influence on those born into it. Systems are designed to benefit those who have designed it. Subjects of these systems rarely benefit, never even getting a fraction of the bounty created off of their efforts.

For example, let's create an "imaginary scenario." Leroy Brown was born in a country where a certain race of people constructed a system to ensure that they are the dominant race. This race has the scarcity mentality and believes that there's only so much of this or that resource to go around so they ensure that most (almost all) of the resources go to them. They ensure that the laws benefit the dominant race. Even in advertisements and media, the dominant race is glorified and the others is vilified. The power structure in this "imaginary country" makes it hard for the inferior race to work and earn a livable wage. So those that are vilified, after a long while, give up on the hopes that the system will ever be fair to them and they start to rob and steal in order to get what they need to live. This in turn gives validity to what the dominant race has been espousing concerning the inferior race. A perfect picture is painted that the inferior race is worthless and shifty. The dominant race then uses talk radio and television shows to create a nationwide atmosphere of hate and aggression against the inferior race to make them submissively stay in their place. Even in the educational system of this "imaginary country," the history of the dominant race is glorified while the history of the inferior is excluded or only when it's fitting, shown in a negative light. Now, as far as the dominant race is concerned, when one person of the inferior race does something wrong, then it's a reflection of the entire race instead of just the actions of that one individual. The dominant race cannot afford to see the perpetrator as an individual because after all, there is nothing good about the entire race. The dominant race may kill those of the inferior race at will with impunity and no one really cares. In their own self-interest, the dominant race will keep this system going by whatever means they have, overtly or covertly. Now if this scenario were real, I would consider the dominant race to possess a demonic genius! This would be pimping and hustling at its finest. I would love to believe that this "imaginary country" doesn't exist. I would be refreshed that people are more humane than what I described. Smile.

Anyway, the point I tried to make in the story was that not only do we as imperfect people have an effect on one another, but the system(s) we're born into has an even larger impact. That being said, running into someone else's game is inevitable or highly likely to say the least. I know that this all may sound fatalistic, but there is hope.

One option to escape the game is to form your own culture that runs opposite to the one you may currently find yourself in. One that runs on different rules and standards - rules that make people more important than the acquisition of things; rules that honor the individual instead of making the individual an object to conquer and subjugate for one's own pleasure. Oops, sorry Jesus, you already did that awhile back. I have to admit that the whole counter-culture idea was a good one. Problem is God, these people down here don't seem to want to do it Your way. Smile.

GIVING UP THE GAME

Listen. Since I brought Jesus up, let's take a look at what happened to him when He went against the grain - to opt out of this destructive manmade system that left people dejected, torn, undervalued and unappreciated. No doubt that dude was lonely. The bible refers to him as a man of sorrows. Anytime you don't want to play the game, look to experience some loneliness for a period of time. Being alone is one of the hardest things for most people. My wife and I know people that go from relationship to relationship without a break in between because they basically never got to know themselves. These poor souls find their value and worth in "belonging to someone else." It's hard for them to go to bed alone at night, thus leaving themselves wide open for game. To many people, being right and sacrificing a little comfort isn't as important as feeling good. A bunch of sensitive sissies killed Jesus because the hard truths He came with hurt their feelings and threatened their way of life and dominance. The lifestyle of the people at the top set the system up to benefit themselves. It was in jeopardy because if Jesus' ideology and teachings caught on, it would make things too equal. If everyone lived like He was trying to tell them, everything would have probably been cool.

So the game is everywhere - from the block, to the bedroom, to the high seats of government. I was a salesman for many years and most of the psychological tricks to get a person to say yes works in the game of love (or lust) as well. The more aware you are of game all around you, the freer you are. The reason you purchased this book is because you want freedom - freedom to make your own choices and to not feel like a pawn in someone else's game.

What you need to realize is that you already have what it takes to set yourself free of the game. Let me put you up on some information. I came from the streets where people are running game 24/7. I recognize game when I see it the majority of the time. When I wanted to go legit and leave hustling behind me, I got into sales because it felt natural to me. I would read sales books and other types of books to gain a psychological advantage over customers and competition. To my surprise, many of the techniques described in those books were things I was already doing... and it was effective. The books I read simply helped me put the right terminology to the techniques.

I said all of that to say that if you look at your life and examine it closely and carefully, you will see many things that you've learned along the way. If applied, it will help you gain what you desire the most - freedom. You don't have to be some street-wise person to recognize game. I'm here to assist you in rediscovering some of the things you already know, but just may not have the clear terminology or systematic approach to effectively combat the game when it comes at you full throttle.

As you read this book, remember two things. Be very observant and trust your first instincts. I learned this from OG's (Original Gangstas) on the street. Whenever I strayed from that advice, I suffered. I've seen people first-hand who knew nothing at all about psychology nor had any experience from "Hood College" that could run circles around people and could read people well enough to recognize game using these two principles alone.

Knowledge is power and the more informed you are, the better you will become at anything. Welcome to a new perspective on game. I hope that the rest of this book will be a real eye-opener for all who read it. I hope to deliver on my promise to enlighten you to the ways of a gamer. After all, I should know because I'm "Eric Durham: Florida's Con-fidence Man." If you want to know more about my days as a con-gamer, go to Amazon.com and purchase the video of the aforementioned title.

<u>NOTES</u>

CHAPTER 3

PLAYA FROM THE HIMALAYAS

Most people don't realize that there are several types of players out there. Because of this, they will fall for the game of one of these players who come along. So before we get into the nuts and bolts of manipulation and how it works, I want to use this chapter to wet your whistle (as the old folks used to say) and introduce some of the players you may be familiar with or will one day encounter.

Folks, knowledge is power. You need to be aware of the types of players out there so you don't fall for the ones that look at relationships as a game to be won. There is an old saying that states, "Game recognizes game." However, the really good players don't rely on one particular technique or angle. They use various techniques which enables them to morph into anything they believe the person wants them to be. The following are a few of the many types of male players and how they engage in play.

1. The Smooth Operator: This player is confident (or at least puts on an air of confidence). He has a good taste in clothing and believes that the clothes

make the man. He is aware that it is important to make a good first impression and that when you look sharp, people usually give you more respect than you would normally get. He studies people and has realized that even since grade school, people judge you by your appearance. This person may have no substance or depth to them, but that won't matter once he gets your emotions involved. After that, you'll make excuses for him and for being with him.

2. The Jerk: This player likes to constantly tease and insult women - always talking trash. His game works particularly well on younger women ages 18-23. By the time they get older, they're tired of his cockiness. He is a master at getting one-night stands, but unfortunately he can never get much more than that because they realize he's a total jerk. They realize he wouldn't really want to take things further anyway.

3. The Baller, Shot-Caller: This guy likes to spend a lot of money and is flashy. He goes out clubbing with his high-rolling friends trying to be cool. My partners and I used to behave like this by looking fresh and throwing money all over the place. Money takes the place of game and the baller gets on with "money-friendly" women at the club.

4. The Direct Player: This player doesn't waste time. He'll be the one going up to women at a

social event giving some preliminary conversation, perhaps offering the young lady a late night dinner at his place. If she declines his offer, it's on to the next young lady because he knows it's all a numbers game.

5. The Popular Player: This guy was more than likely the football or basketball star in high school or college and has a reputation for sleeping with many women. Believe it or not, this is actually a turn-on for a lot of women. He could be popular for the way he dressed or anything. It doesn't really matter for what reason he became popular as long as enough women in the area (city, town, college) have heard about him. He really doesn't have a lot of game and is only riding on his popular status. Once his popularity disappears, he's going to have a hard time scoring.

6. Slick Willy: This player gets on with women by lying to them about all the interesting things he does, has done, or is about to do. Some of it may be true, however, many things are stretched. He's a good conversationalist and can make girls laugh and feel good. He makes girls think that he's an awesome guy even though he most likely is not.

7. The Online Pimp: This player likes to surf the dating sites. He makes an awesome profile that doesn't reveal much about him. He chooses his best pictures for his profile, creates an eyebrow-

raising first message, and sends it out to as many women in his age group (or younger) on all the major dating sites. He lets his fingers do the macking. After a limited number of replies, he finally manages to meet up with a woman that doesn't look anything close to her profile pictures either. He'll still try to have sex with her, though. This player is trying to fish for something easy. Trying to hook-up on the internet is less threatening than live face-to-face encounters. I would say that this player's game is in the weak range.

8. The Pusher Man: When I think of this player, I think of that old Curtis Mayfield song. This player knows that there are many women who love to "party," so he casually drops hints while laying down his game to them. When his target bites, this player starts to exaggerate all the more about his stash and his crib. The woman really doesn't care as long as there's at least some of the party treats he promised there when they get to his place. He doesn't need much game, but when the dope is gone, his game is too.

9. The Business Player: This player describes himself as a business owner or partner of a multimillion dollar company when in actuality, he's just a network marketer selling the latest juice, powder, pill, body wrap, legal, or

telecommunications service, etc. This fellow is very ambitious and has fully bought into the philosophy of the company he works for. This gives him sort of an attractive flare. You will know this player by certain catch phrases like "JOB = just over broke" or "I'm close to winning this Mercedes Benz and trip to the Bahamas because of all of my hard work in recruiting new members into this ground-breaking company. I want you to come with me on the trip." Many have been taken by this player's energy and enthusiasm. This player dresses for success as if he is going into his plush office within a fortune 500 company when in actuality, he's going to drop off some flyers to all of the corner stores in the hood hoping someone calls believing in the dream as he has. Usually within a few months, he'll be excited about another "million dollar opportunity." I should have called this guy the financially unsecure player.

9. The Dirty Player: This guy will do anything to get back to a woman's place after a social event. He knows that once he's in the house, he has a greater chance of having sex with his mark. He'll tell the woman that he missed his ride and his buddy's phone is out of service or he lost his keys to his house and won't be able to get a locksmith until the morning or any sort of excuse that will appeal to a woman's emotional side. This dude's

game is weak and his antics show desperation, but this is hidden from the unsuspecting woman.

BUSTING THE LADIES

I can't just let all the men get the exposure now. I also have to give up the game about women for my dudes who may have picked up a copy of this book. This one is for you, fellas.

Women are the most subtle creatures on earth and many are playing the game just like men. Men want sex, but on the other hand, women players use sex as a as a tool to get things like favors, money, dinner, etc. A female player will usually have no less than four to five guys in her little black book because she will use each of them for something different. For example, one will pay her rent. Another will pay her car note. Yet another will finance her cell phone bill. Keep in mind that a good female player will not have to have sex with any of the guys.

How can you spot a female player? Here are some of her traits;

- She can be indifferent. You will see her have more of a "take it or leave it" attitude.

- She's intelligent. Her intelligence really intrigues men, who, like women, enjoy a challenge.

- She's a master tease. She knows how to keep your interest while giving in only enough to keep you around.

- She's flirtatious. She knows how to dress in order to keep your attention without appearing trashy or desperate.

- She spreads her hustle. She can be compared to a gold digger, but she spreads her hustle, meaning that instead of staying with one man and taking all of the money out of his pockets, this female player has several men at a time, balancing what she gets. With her, you have to pay to play.

- She won't show you affection in public. Why? Because one of her other men could happen to see her with someone else and she also doesn't want to ruin any chances with other men who could be watching.

- She's popular. Her phone may ring off the hook while you're with her, but if you notice, she always screens them in your presence.

- She usually takes charge of the conversation and any situation. She will ask all the right questions and try to make all the plans.

- She is usually the dominant one out of her crew. If you are observant, you will see her girlfriends hanging off of her every word. The female player will also dictate a lot to her friends as well.

- She knows what guys want. She is very observant like the male player, trying to find any weakness she can play on.

There is an old saying that tells people that if they want to learn the game, then they should talk to women. This is true. I have had many female friends school me on how women think and operate. Many times, my mouth would drop when they would tell me how treacherous, cunning, and deceitful a woman can be. I thank God for them because I was spared a lot of unnecessary heartache, as I was always one to wear my emotions on my sleeve. When I was younger, I believed every smiling face that would come my way. I think "green" would be the proper word for my mindset at that time.

Regardless of all of that, what men need to know is that when we are in our rightful place, women will naturally follow. When I say rightful place, I mean respecting ourselves and others; seeing ourselves as teachers, protectors, lovers and providers of our families; having a vision for our lives and families; and anchoring our life in God. When a man rises to his rightful place, the games will end.

GIVING UP THE GAME

In the next section, we are going to get to the player mechanics - how manipulation works and how players use it to their advantage.

Now it's time to buckle your seatbelts.

<u>NOTES</u>

GIVING UP THE GAME

CHAPTER 4

CAN YOU SPOT A LIE?

If you cannot spot a lie, you'll never be able to recognize game with a high level of accuracy. There are many who are comfortable with lying. In fact, in order to get over on people, you have to practice lying until you become believable. When a person gets to that level of mastery, getting away with things becomes addictive. When I was in the con game, whether it was creating and selling fake temporary paper tags and vehicle registrations; starting fake companies and cashing payroll checks at banks; or assuming another person's identity and getting state identification in that person's name, I was always cool, calm, and collected.

A movie that I really enjoyed reminded me of the things I did back in the mid to late 90's. That movie was *Catch Me If You Can* starring Leonardo DiCaprio. Besides the James Bond series, this was one of my favorite movies. This movie, based on the true story of Frank Abagnale Jr., who, before his 19th birthday, successfully conned millions of dollars worth of checks as a Pan Am pilot, doctor, and legal prosecutor.

GIVING UP THE GAME

Now, I never made it to the point of making millions (not even close), but the ability for me to run game and acquire the things that I did was more exhilarating than the money itself.

If you desire to spot a con, you have to know what to look for. Many people hold on to notions like if a person can't look you in the eye, fidget too much, or any number of identifiers, then they're lying. I'm here to set the record straight to help you gain more proficiency in your lie-detecting skills. For example, let's explore the notion that a person must be truthful if they look you in the eye. There are many people that are simply shy or who have low self-esteem that may not look people in the eye for any prolonged period of time. Many people with high self-esteem rarely use the oppressive stare-down type of eye contact. Because of this faulty belief that a majority of people have concerning eye contact, I was consistently able to deceive and milk thousands of dollars from people on a daily basis. I learned to put aside any fidgety inclinations in order to appear calm. Before I would initiate a scheme, I would create a script like I would for a sales presentation. I went over it until my body exuded a calm confidence. At that point, I was able to implement the plan almost flawlessly.

GIVING UP THE GAME

I realize that I may have made this process appear overly simplistic, but in the next chapter, you'll see some of the techniques that have to be put into play for a game/con to actually work.

There is something called a baseline which is a concept made popular by body language expert Janine Driver.

You must know a person's baseline in order to be able to truly evaluate if they're lying. What exactly is a baseline? A baseline is the persons modus operandi, or to put it in English, mode of operation. How does the person operate under normal stimuli? This may require you to spend a little time with your target. Note to yourself how the person responds when first meeting someone; what their normal tone of voice is; are they normally a fidgety person; do they normally give good eye contact or not; or do they normally give a lot or a little detail when they are responding to a question? What you are looking for is any deviation from their normal behavior, their baseline. You have to learn to question everything, even the small things that seem inconsequential. I'm in no way trying to make people paranoid and non-trusting, but you have to be careful and trust your instincts.

There is a quote that many business leaders borrowed from our 40th president Ronald Regan,

"Trust, but verify." So even when you do trust someone, it's always a smart move to check up on them as much as you can. There is too much at stake no not be cautious - things like your life, health, financial wellbeing, and so on.

The best way to get a good read of anyone is to make sure you establish rapport with them first. In order to establish rapport, you have to use body language that appears non-threatening, open, and warm. You want the person to relax around you as much as possible. Also, allow the other person to talk as much as possible while keeping an eye on their body movements. Remember, people love to talk about themselves. Most times when you're talking, they are just waiting for you to finish talking so that they can get back to what interests them the most, themselves. These are human weaknesses that you can exploit to your advantage if you need to. I would never advocate using the few tactics I'm giving in this book for anyone to use in a predatory way - only as a way to get needed information to protect your best asset... you. Remember this, liars are always trying to convince you of something, but truthful people aim only to convey information.

Albert Mehrabian was a researcher of body language in the 1950's. He found that the total impact of a message is about seven percent verbal (words only), 38 percent vocal (including tone of voice, inflection, and other sounds), and 55 percent nonverbal.

Like Mehrabian, anthropologist Ray Birdwhistell found that the verbal component of a face-to-face conversation is less than 35 percent which leaves over 65 percent of communication to be conveyed nonverbally. Studies of thousands of recorded sales interviews and negotiations during the 1970's and 1980's showed that, in business encounters, body language accounts for between 60 and 80 percent of the impact made around a negotiating table.

So as you can see, a deceiver has more tools in his or her arsenal than conversation alone. Good deceivers are like good salesmen, but great deceivers are like politicians. Smile.

<u>NOTES</u>

CHAPTER 5

MANIPULATION: RECOGNIZING GAME

Okay, here's the chapter you've been dying to get to. Hopefully you've read the preceding chapters and didn't skip ahead to this one. By the end of this chapter, the inexperienced will be able to recognize someone coming with game from a mile away and the experienced will be able to articulate the things they inwardly knew, but didn't know how to put into words. Let's get right to it, shall we?

I will begin by asking this question, "What do leaders and deceivers have in common?" Come on, you can do it! I know you have the answer... You don't know? Okay. Let me tell you. Both the leader and the deceiver have influence. The difference between a leader and a deceiver is that a leader uses his/her influence to enrich and benefit everyone he/she is influencing while the deceiver is using his/her influence to enrich or benefit himself/herself to the detriment of others.

Our nations' military understands the power of influence and uses it as a weapon when engaging our nation's enemies. I once read that influence operations are focused on affecting the perceptions and behaviors of leaders, groups, or entire populations. Influence operations employ capabilities to affect behaviors, protect operations, communicate commander's intent, and project accurate information to achieve desired effects across the cognitive domain. These effects should result in differing behavior or a change in the adversary's decision cycle, which aligns with the commander's objectives. The military's capabilities of influence are in actuality psychological operations.

There is a science to manipulation. According to research, people are more likely to analyze information more carefully when they have both the desire <u>and</u> the ability to analyze it carefully (Petty, Cacioppo, & Godman, 1981). The pace of modern life is not allowing us to make fully thoughtful decisions (Cohen, 1979; Milgram, 1970). Sometimes life issues are very complicated; time is so limited, mental fatigue so high, distractions so intense, and emotions so all over the place so much so that a person is in no condition to operate mindfully.

We exist in a very complex environment and as a result, humans deal with information by using shortcuts because we simply don't have the capacity, energy or time to analyze all of the aspects in each event, situation and person we consistently encounter. Stereotyped behavior is prevalent in human interaction because it is the most efficient form of behaving (Gigerenzer & Goldstein, 1996).

These mental shortcuts are helpful because we have predefined "identifiers" for people, places and things. For instance, the news may have relayed information that the east side of town has a lot of drug trafficking in that area. With this information in hand, you don't need to over-analyze the situation. So, for instance, when you are trying to go home from your night shift at work, you simply take another route just to be safe. You don't need to analyze what streets in that neighborhood are safe. You don't need to say to yourself that not everyone in that neighborhood is involved in illegal activity. You simply just avoid it.

This human tendency to use shortcuts can be used to manipulate people as follows. People usually trust authority figures. One of our shortcuts is that if a person has some sort of fancy badge, has "Dr." in front of their name, or holds some sort of official sounding title, we assume that they have received the proper training, are culturally competent and compassionate, and have the public's best interest at heart.

People have been abused, misused, mistreated and sometimes worse because of this way of automatic, stereotyped behavior. So although life moves fast, we have to find a way to slow down and be more discerning, cautious and wise in our dealings with others.

The first step in recognizing game is to realize that as humans, we all have weaknesses that can be exploited. The better you know yourself, you are less likely to become a victim to someone else's game. Like Socrates said, "Man, know thyself." Another example of human weakness is the belief that certain people will never do anything to hurt us. Many times in a love relationship between man and woman or even between two friends, we can deceive ourselves into believing that an unfaithful friend or mate is faithful even with obvious signs that display the contrary.

THE PRINCIPLE OF SOCIAL PROOF

What the heck is social proof? Social proof is a psychological phenomenon where people assume the actions of others reflect correct behavior for a given situation. This effect is most pronounced in uncertain situations where the correct course is not easy to determine and therefore is determined by looking at what other people do. Social proof is also known as herd behavior.

GIVING UP THE GAME

Imagine you're at a theme park and you see two rollercoaster rides next to each other. In one line, you see a bunch of people waiting for their turn to ride. In the line for the other ride, there are only two people in it. Which one do you ride? You'll most likely ride the one with the long line because your thought will most likely be that the ride with only two people in line is straight wack!

This example was chosen to highlight one concept of social proof. Since you have the gist of it, let me show you how men and women use this principle to get noticed. Say you go out to a social event with a few friends. Physically position yourself in the center of them. The person in the center of a group is the focal point and subsequently gets the most attention.

Guys, go out with some female friends to have a good time. Other women won't realize these are just your friends and they will be more attracted to you when they see other women interested in you.

I remember back in the day while hanging out with my friends at Club Atlanta, chilling with a few female friends and my homeboys. I got some play from this attractive female just because she saw a female leaning over to me laughing and having a good time. I learned something new that night.

Ladies, make sure you are in the center of a few friends and that you are the most attractive out of your entourage. You'll have many men wanting some of your time.

Remember, you are rated by the people around you. When using the principle of social proof, fans are better than friends. If you can get people saying your name and clamoring around you like you're some superstar, you'll go far when it comes to seduction. Take nothing at face value. There's an old saying, "Trust half of what you see and none of what you hear."

THE PRINCIPLE OF COMMITMENT AND CONSISTENCY

Humans, by nature, have a desire to be and appear consistent with what we have already done. This trait, like many others, can be easily exploited. Knowing this principle has helped many get a foot-in-the-door. Theodore Newcomb (1953) viewed the desire to be consistent as a central motivator for behavior. To get a person to agree to a large request, all you have to do is have the person agree to a series of small requests first. The more a person goes along with small requests or commitments, the more likely they are to continue in the direction you want them to go. In fact, they will feel obligated to go along with larger requests later on. Here is an example entrapment phrase, "Come on... just let me take you to lunch just one time. I just want to get to know you a little better." When this small request is agreed to, a bond between the one asking and the one being asked is created. Even though the person may only have agreed out of politeness, a bond is still made nonetheless. When the young lady in this example attempts to justify her decision to go out with this guy, she may now have a genuine feeling of closeness with him or at the very least, a heightened interest in him at this point. Now when he makes a future request, she will feel obliged to act consistently with her earlier decision.

This psychological trick is working on me right now as I write this book. I've committed to giving you the game, so I feel obligated to be consistent with that commitment.

THE PRINCIPLE OF LIKING

Researchers have found evidence that women like men more when they were led to believe that the men like them. All you have to do is drum it up a bit and this tactic, like the others, can get you in the door. It works on men as well as women. This brings to mind a girl I used to have an on-and-off relationship with when I was in my 20's. She stayed in a nearby community and was very attractive. When we got together, she made me feel like there was no one else in the world but me. She had an ability to make a person feel special without seeming too needy or eager to please. Like the cereal commercial, I was "coo-coo for Cocoa Puffs" for a brief period of time. I just couldn't get her out of my system it seemed. Whether she had someone or I had someone, we would creep with each other and then lose contact for a year or so at a time. It was weird. But then, one day after catching up with her and doing our usual, the thrill was gone. I thought to myself at that moment that she was just an average chick. I wondered why I was always going crazy over her. Well, I actually had my answer already. By this time, I'd become good at spotting game and running game. I still liked her, but I wasn't "green" anymore in the sense that I refused to let myself fall head over heels for her or anyone else for that matter.

Let me share with you some of her game that my game radar picked up on.

THE SCARCITY PRINCIPLE

She was elusive and had an air mystery about her. She would make me chase her and then finally give in. She never made it too easy, but at the same time never made it too hard. I tried a couple of times to "lock her down" and make it official, but she wasn't having it. She knew she was a catch. Every dude I knew was trying to get with her. I was happy just to have a piece of her whenever I could.

GIVING UP THE GAME

She made herself a woman who was rare. A person using the scarcity tactic can cause people to act or react with clouded judgment and end up chasing something that they can never possess.

We all know that whatever is rare or expensive is heavily sought after. The more we are seen, the more we do, the more we come across as ordinary. When something has limited availability, people assign it more value. People want more of what they cannot have. The gamer will explain that they can give you what no one else will, whether it's adventure or whatever. In subtle indirect ways, you are made to believe that not being with them is a great loss.

There are two reasons why the scarcity principle works; 1) when things are difficult to get, they are usually more valuable so that can make it appear to have better quality; and 2) when things become less available, we could lose the chance to acquire them altogether. When this happens, we assign the scarce service, item or person more value because they are harder to acquire.

If you're part of some civic group, community club or other organization, stay away for a while and you'll see that people will talk about you more. They may even admire you more. Practice absence. The weapon of scarcity will increase your value.

GIVING UP THE GAME

THE PRINCIPLE OF RECIPROCITY

The principle of reciprocity states that when a person provides us with something, we attempt to repay him or her in kind. Reciprocation produces a sense of obligation which can be a powerful tool in persuasion.

Ok. Now that I have shared the definition, let me just say how funny it is when a guy takes a girl to the movies and dinner and think that the reciprocity principle with get him into her bed. Trying to use this principle the wrong way has backfired on many.

When you're just meeting a person of interest and start spending a lot of money on them immediately, they will start to feel uncomfortable and back away because they don't want to be trapped into feeling obligated to you for anything.

So what I used to do is to make them feel like I didn't expect anything. This worked well for me because I seemed different from the norm which gave room for the principle of reciprocity to do its magic.

So ladies, even though they may seem like they don't have a care in the world and don't need you for anything, you still have to watch it. The principle of reciprocity is already at work and if you're not careful, you can "get got" fairly easy.

GIVING UP THE GAME

You may not give it up as easy as this one girl I got with once, but keep your eyes open. I took a woman to Burger King and bought her a burger and shake. Within minutes, I hit it in the park in my car. Before dropping her off, I took the shake back. Yeah, I hope none of you are like that!

Hopefully, now you are more enlightened to game. Though everyone is unique, we all have things inherent in our makeup that makes us vulnerable to game. Be watchful.

NOTES

CHAPTER 6

APPLYING MY GAME

My game was really simple. I would get the ladies laughing so hard that before they knew it, their panties were off and they're asking the next morning, "What happened? Wait... Did we...?" I'd reply something crazy like "Yeah chick, we just knocked dirty, nasty undignified, filthy, raunchy boots and your pets were watching too. Now get on in that kitchen and make me some eggs and grits. And don't burn my toast!" At this time, I'd usually find myself outside her house in my boxers with all of my clothes being thrown at me while the neighbors looked and laughed me to my car. It was hard being a broke-down pimp.

Just joking, family. Seriously though, getting a woman to lighten up and have a good time always worked for me. I didn't have any sense, y'all! I just didn't care. Even when they couldn't stand me, they still would deal with me. I literally had this one girl who would tell me how much she couldn't stand me. A few minutes later, she would ask me what I was doing later on. I'd tell her something slick like, "I'll be in your bed watching TV after I knock the dust off that thang. Girl, don't act like you don't know!"

A lot of people I know lead their approach with flattery. You have to know when to use it, though. I rarely, if ever, lead with flattery for two reasons; 1) I aim to first get their defenses down. For it to be really effective, get her to a place where you can sense that she's digging you at least a little bit; 2) So many women have heard flattery that it's gotten tired and old. Good-looking women know they look good so tell them something they don't know already. You can't walk up to a girl talking about, "Girl you know you're fine. Gimme your number." You're setting yourself up to get laughed at.

The reason I didn't care about what women thought and would clown them because my homeboys, Jeff and Ron, told me something a long time ago that I would never forget. They told me that women want sex as just much as guys do. They try to pretend like they don't because they don't want men calling them whores.

So from that point on, I thought of it like in the *Matrix* movie where the main character, Neo, got to a point where he could read the code behind the matrix. He was no longer distracted by the wiles that the smoke screen displayed. I felt that I could finally see through all the bull. Women needed to simply stop playing and give me what I wanted.

GIVING UP THE GAME

A funny thing happened. I found out that when you could read a woman, they can sense that you can see right through them. A majority of their defenses would just come down after that point. This made it easier for me to have sex with them. The thrill of conquering different types of women became addictive. With each conquest, I felt like the man, superior. I felt attractive and no longer the poor ugly kid no one liked. The successful conquests made me feel validated. I felt desired and valuable like I was worth something to people. To me, this was what mattered. I wasn't just screwing around with the ladies, I was screwing myself with the foolish way I thought about myself. I had a really messed up outlook on life.

All I can say is that I thank Jesus that He preserved me when I was out there wilding out. He's protected me from catching sexually transmitted diseases. Dis-ease was, in truth, what I truly had. I was certainly not at ease with the person I was. The women, clubbing, and drinking only masked my inner feelings.

In the black community, many of us deal with depression, psychosis, post-traumatic stress disorder, and other mental and emotional issues that we don't seek help for. We are either too prideful to seek help or just can't afford the treatment and counseling sessions. The one outlet we do have in our poverty and issue-filled communities is the local church. There are many competent pastors who provide excellent counseling for free. Just throwing that out there just in case there's anyone reading this who is as crazy as I was. We need to know when we should take ourselves somewhere to get our head worked on. Ha!

I like to laugh and try not to take myself too seriously. I hate being stiff and boring. At the end of the day, I've discovered that we are all more similar than we give ourselves credit. Many people are just uptight because they have allowed life experiences to make them that way. I would often come into a woman's life to serve as comic relief. I could change it up and be serious if the situation or person called for it because my preferred approach didn't work with everyone.

It's a numbers thing. Some women are looking for someone tall or someone short (not sure when that is the case). Some are looking for a roughneck while others want an athlete. Some have it already worked out in their minds exactly how they want a man to approach them even down to the exact words they want to hear. They have determined their own give-in point. Some women are looking for a fraternity man. The list is endless. Let me give you an example. I joined a particular fraternity. The initiation period was three months long. A funny observation was that these guys would dog out all of the initiates on line together. I thought at the time it was worth it. I loved the brotherhood, comradery, and commitment to community service.

During the second month of my initiation period, my friend (who recruited me) and another brother went to eat at the International House of Pancakes (IHOP). I was made to carry their umbrellas. Just as I was about to walk through the front doors, one of the guys said, "Whoa, what do you think you're doing? You'd better wait until we walk through first." So when we got to the table, there was this one fine young lady I had always wanted to talk to in school, but she never gave me the time of day. There was another woman with her. As I started to sit down, the same brother said, "You'd better not sit down until I tell you to sit down." So there I was, embarrassed and looking like a complete punk. Man, if he wasn't a brother and we were in the street, I would've decked dude right in the mouth for trying me in front of those women. He was playing me like I was soft.

I joked a lot, but my friends knew I had a hot head at times and was known for setting it off. But, I submitted to my up-line. So of course, I had to order last. Oh my goodness! Thinking back on all this, it was crazy. Anyway, the brothers were telling the women who were in the sister sorority about the new round of initiates and that I was one of them. So the woman who wouldn't give me the time of day in high school blurted out, "Oh yea, I know Eric. He and I go way back." I was like, "What?" I didn't know this girl even knew my name! I made a mental note as to how people are so fake. I did like that she knew my name, though. Ha!

That goes to show you that people can be moved by some of anything. Because people are so caught up with status, titles, image and appearance, it makes them susceptible to all kinds of game. This is why Hollywood stars and musicians stay employed. Needless to say, being in this organization blew my head up big time. It was never quite right, though. I would go through times where I was high, super confident and all. Then I would go through periods where I didn't think well of myself at all. People could tell it when they looked at me.

During the times I felt confident, I scored with the ladies a majority of the time. When I was down in the dumps, nothing would work. There is something about confidence that is attractive. But more than being confident, being whole is far more attractive. There are many books about confidence, but I haven't ran across as many that talks about being whole.

If I was whole at that time, I don't think I would have been trying to sleep my way into happiness if you get my meaning. The game is for chumps who haven't figured out who they are as a person. I like sex like the next man, but what I was doing with the rest of my homeboys was just unhealthy in so many ways.

My advice to current players is to do what one of my friends did. He went to counseling and found out that many women that he thought he was running game on had some serious hurts they were dealing with and just wanted to feel loved. Many women will trade their bodies to fill a void in their lives. They may have not received the love they should have from their fathers at home or they may have been sexually abused and have confused sex with love. In truth, most of the "game" guys think that they're running isn't game at all. Whether they know it or not, their game is preying on the weak. A lot of times girls will game on you and make you feel like they can't resist your advances. In actuality, they wanted to have sex with you anyway. They leave you walking away, beating your chest like King Kong, when in fact, you just got played, son.

I'll put you up on some more game before I end this chapter. Here is another tactic that is virtually simple. I had success playing the friend role. I was always around, always listening and showing myself sympathetic and helpful. Then one day, when they get horny or their man does them wrong, I was the shoulder for them to cry on. They would tell me, "I wish all men were sensitive like you." I'd then turn on the humor and say something stupid like, "Girl, if all men were like me, this world would be an almost perfect place." After that, it was a wrap.

Let me see if you've been learning since you've been reading this book. If you miss this point I'm about to bring out, you need to reread a few of the previous chapters. This is an example of how I cashed in while playing the friend role. This particular young lady was running game too. She wanted to "get got" as the expression goes. She was hoping that I would have a comeback that would make her feel comfortable to go further.

It will start with her coming on to me. We start kissing and I'd come out with, "Oh, my! What are you doing?" She'd respond, "Yeah, right. You know you want this." Ha! Dang skippy I wanted it. As much time as I put in playing the friend role, waiting around for her to slip, I feel like she owed me big time. I expected her to pay up. I'd follow up with more stupid comments like, "If this is what will make you feel better, you can have my body. I'm only doing this for you."

Since I'm telling on myself, I have to be truthful and say that this really wasn't game all of the time because I've always, to use street vernacular, had the Captain-save-a-whore mentality. Yes folks, men have this built in knight in shining armor complex that makes us vulnerable to game no matter how much game when know or have used. So men, be very careful because you cannot beat women at the game if they choose to play simply because they are far more subtle than men. If a woman who wants to run game goes and put on a tight red dress that shows a little cleavage, half of the wannabe so-called players would be knocked out of the box, drooling like little puppy dogs at first meeting. Most of the game I learned, I learned from women telling me how they are. So what does that tell you?

My intent when writing this chapter was not to make myself look like some smooth Casanova who've slept with hundreds of women because that's definitely not the case. But, I wanted to bring out the fact that there are obvious things that can cause you to fall into the trap of someone's game if you're not careful. If a person can move you from rational thinking into the emotional realm, you've lost and they've won. So don't lose.

NOTES

<u>NOTES</u>

CHAPTER 7

BLINDSIDED

I once found myself in an emotional relationship with a young woman who was a friend to me and my wife and I almost lost my marriage. How in the world could I have let this happen, let alone even see it coming, especially since I know game and have run game many times?

Let me tell you how it all started. My wife and I allowed our relationship to grow stale. Everything the other did seemed to get on the other's nerves. Neither of us where giving the other the things that would have built the other up. We neglected each other's emotional and physical needs and desires.

I was ready to call it quits...for real. But I was holding on for dear life even though I felt like I was dying inside. I've turned down many opportunities to cheat. I've removed myself from situations that could have led to unfaithfulness on several occasions. Because I was not where I needed to be spiritually and emotionally, I let my guard down on this one.

This mutual friend and I would talk about just about everything. Mistake one. She would reveal a lot of personal stuff. I would share some of my frustrations with my wife and she would share frustrations about her boyfriend. She would flatter me and be very deliberate in letting me know how she treats the men she's courting. She would seal it with comments boasting how she didn't know why my wife treated me the way I had revealed. She was very aware of the issues I had with my wife in our relationship. Mistake two.

It felt good venting as I would hold a lot of stuff in. My wife and I had gotten to a place where we couldn't talk without it being a big blow-out. So I just stopped sharing with her. The mutual friend would say things that would build me up. She would normally invite me stay and talk longer whenever I tried to leave. I had a false sense of safety with her because we usually talked in a public place.

I started feeling like this woman understood me. She would laugh at all of my jokes and always showed that she was interested in what was going on with me. The friendly hugs would last longer than they should have and our bodies became closer than they should have been.

Now before you think to yourself that I'm trying to make myself out to be the innocent victim, think again. There came a point where I felt it in my gut that I was really messing up – that I should proceed no further...cut it off. But by that time, I was already emotionally invested. I started making overt advances and there came a point where going to the next level was on the table if you know what I mean.

I don't know if she realized it or not, but her behavior was classic of one of the average gamer. Let's break this down. 1) She was a good listener. 2) She consistently made comments about my attractiveness. 3) She effectively played the damsel in distress which few men have been able to resist. 4) She exalted her positive traits against my wife's negative traits. 5) She showed herself available to me. 6) She blatantly advertised her desire to have a man with the qualities I possessed.

Of course, these signs are obvious and elementary. A person who claims to know game like I do and even has the audacity to write a book about game should have seen this coming a mile away. But I was blinded by rage, obsessing about my own estimation of the pitifulness of my marriage. This left me open for subtle manipulation. It isn't hard to manipulate someone who wants to be manipulated. Simply put, I liked the attention.

We never took the situation further, but we were both guilt-ridden for allowing ourselves to be so treacherous and evil. We both backed away from each other in our everyday dealings and tried to forget everything. She didn't want to hurt my wife and asked me not to say anything.

Instead of focusing on my wife's needs and desires, I was focusing on myself and allowing myself to get to a state of mind that has ruined many marriages. On the front wind, I felt good that I was able to back away from a situation that many would have pressed to the max. I reflected on what got me to that place in my marriage and committed to making serious adjustments in my life.

A few weeks later, I ended up telling my wife. The guilt was too much. But it was more than guilt. I secretly wanted my wife to realize that she needed to tighten up. I don't want to be the last thing on her to-do list. Pay attention to me, woman! Don't take me for granted! Someone else would be happy to be with me! I know, so immature. Boy, I behaved like a bratty jerk especially when she had equally legitimate gripes about me and how I treated her.

I calculated that when I told her, she would either take notice which would hopefully cause us to put some serious effort into our marriage (basically act the way I wanted her to) or we would divorce. Well my, poorly thought-out scheme got us to the point where we were really about to divorce.

It took some serious prayer, marriage counseling, intervention (divine and natural) and space, eating of pride, begging, and pleading. Thank God I got her back! I started being less demanding, more understanding, more patient and overlooked things that I used to blew up about prior to this situation.

I ended up being the one who realized where change needed to start...with me. I needed to take a good, hard look at the man in the mirror. I needed to not allow anyone outside of myself to anger me to the point where I would react or respond in a manner that betrayed my personal beliefs of faithfulness. Nothing external should cause me not to treat people with respect, love and kindness.

I and my wife's relationship is stronger than ever before these days because I walk with her in a more understanding way. I'm not as demanding and critical as I was before. I forgive quicker and do my best not to feel threatened if she has an opinion that differs from mine. After all, at the end of the day, we are still on the same team...Team Durham.

Men have to lead with love, not manipulation. Our women are reflections of us. If we bring honey to the relationship, we will get it in return. But if we bring vinegar, we will get something sour tasting right back. If my wife has an off-day and is cranky, I just give her space and go and do something else until she's ready to talk instead of trying to "adjust" her so that I don't have to deal with attitudes. I thank God for Mrs. Durham. I'm a better man today because of her.

<u>NOTES</u>

<u>**NOTES**</u>

CHAPTER 8

GREEN PASTURES

Game is everywhere, even on the college campuses all across America. These players are successful so often because of how they are perceived. A guy or girl in college is viewed as having their act together and are above the "ghetto games" of people in the hood who are going nowhere. Their intentions are taken at face value and as pure. So when they approach a fellow college schoolmate whose curiosity and hormones are as high as their own, they give in because of the false sense of trust on a basic level. So the newness of freedom from the rules of home combined with their lack of experience, gives an opportunist college player what they want which is an exciting time with someone hot. Unfortunately, many young scholars leave college pregnant, unable to finish college or having to finish later in life. Others end up with sexually transmitted diseases and many more leave college with wounded spirits and broken hearts that may take years to mend. Hopefully, their hearts will mend around the time they finish paying off their college loans. College students, beware and take care of your best investment... yourself.

Enjoy this account of an experience that a friend had while in college.

GIVING UP THE GAME

JOLLY GREEN FRESHMAN

Graduating high school and then going off to college is certainly an interesting experience. Of all the transitions I've lived through, this one was very significant. Not only was I moving over two hours away from home, I was considered an adult which finally qualified me to make my own decisions.

During my first year of college, I was a typical freshman – naïve, wet behind the ears, green, etc. Since this was the first time I was on my own, I had to determine my own bedtime, how late or early I would stay out, how much money I would spend and for what. It was an exciting, yet confusing time for me, especially when it came to figuring out relationships. Even today, I still have trouble navigating some relationships.

I arrived at the college campus with more than just my clothes, a few pieces of furniture, and $20 in my pocket. I also brought my undiscovered emotional baggage which included the "dark-skin complex." I won't go into the history of how this complex has been perpetuated since American slavery. Simply put, I walked around with an inferior posture whenever I was in any comparison to a fairer- skinned person whether they be a lighter-skinned black woman or white woman. I had friends and associates of all skin complexions, *but I felt the most comfortable around people who had complexions closer to my own. At least I felt we were on the same playing field.*

This concept held truer whenever I went out. Whenever there is an environment where the opposite sex was present, I felt overlooked simply because I wasn't light-skinned. The complexion of a woman's skin said things about her. It's kind of a like a stereotype. Darker-skinned women were associated with being mean and hard which makes them less attractive. On the other hand, fair-skinned black women as well as white women were associated with being easy, nice. Because of this, they seem to be more attractive or a better catch. I didn't make this connection in a cognitive way back then, but I felt it none the less. Men looking for easy prey saw the connection and my resulting behavior.

Having a reduced self-esteem coupled with naiveté made me an easy target for the more insightful player. Being darker-skinned put me in a category where I was most likely not to be approached to be asked for my phone number. No man really wants to work too hard to get a woman, especially if the goal is to have a short-term fling anyway. Most men were looking for a brief, good time. A lengthy courtship was not as appealing. Taking time to woo the likes of a "mean", dark-skinned woman was just not worth it, especially since an easier, much nicer, and faster option was available.

I met my first boyfriend in college while in pursuit of completing a project for one of my classes. No matter what bonehead things I did while in college, my education was always the main thing. One day, one of my classmates and I visited an on-campus museum in order to investigate some art pieces. It was a slow day for the museum because we were one of the only patrons in there. Upon entering, we were greeted by the attendant who was a senior student. My classmate and I took the liberty of having the place to ourselves by giggling and talking loud as we walked throughout the gallery. We would quiet ourselves periodically in order to not disturb the prestigious atmosphere of the gallery. The art pieces were arranged along the walls of a big square room. As we neared the end of the exhibit, my classmate began noticing the attendant repeatedly looking at us. I figured we were being too loud, but she insisted that he was looking more at me. Since she was a lighter-skinned woman from the Caribbean, I just knew she was mistaken. We had been out together before. I knew the drill. She was approached for interest and I usually found myself standing to the side waiting for them to finish talking. She was a very nice girl who was very deliberate about who she'd share her contact information with. I perceived this situation to be the same.

GIVING UP THE GAME

My classmate continued to badger me about the attendant looking at me until we did a little experiment. The idea was for her and I to put some distance between us (to look at different art pieces that were spaced far away from each other.) Then, we could discover which of the two he was really looking at. Once we separated, I discovered that she was right. So much so that the attendant got up from his desk to ask me if I needed any help with anything. I said I was fine and he went back to his seat at the front desk.

My classmate and I got back together to recap the results of the experiment. She gloated about being right and asked me what the attendant and I were talking about. She wondered why she wasn't personally asked if she needed help with anything. We took time to discuss the art pieces and took down a few notes before leaving. On our way out, we thanked the attendant. He proceeded to ask me for my phone number. He behaved as though my classmate wasn't even standing next to me – as though I was the only woman in the room.

In my mind, the attendant was bold. He went down the path less chosen. I was impressed with his willingness to go after the challenge and not take the easy road as I had witnessed men do time after time. At that moment, I was the one preferred for a change. It felt great!

It could have been the very thing he was after, though. Women with the low self-esteem are just as, if not easier than the fairer-skinned ones. They are not used to the attention so they will do anything to keep it on them. Darker-skinned women could have simply been the attendant's preference. I would come to find out that his mother is darker-skinned and his father is lighter-skinned. Or he could have picked up my emotional baggage and decided to make me his mark. Being that he was a bit socially awkward, he needed low-hanging fruit to even get on. Either way, it worked.

I would not come off of my high for at least a few weeks. Our courtship lasted for a few months intermittently. I had become one of those freshmen who had gotten caught up with senior which meant I was good for one thing. In my mind, I was different, though. This man saw me for me and it wasn't a one night stand. It was a real relationship. The only thing he was doing was spending time with me when he wasn't studying. He had no time for anyone else until... I found out differently. Naiveté can be a killer in many ways.

I was and still have a world in which my mind travels to where people should just do and be right. If you say you like someone, let it be true. If you don't, don't say it or lead a person on. Whenever I considered myself in a relationship with a boyfriend, he was the only one I was messing with. Period. I'm still this way today. What I didn't verify at the time was if this was the same philosophy my boyfriend had. I found out the hard way that he really wasn't that into me after a while. After a couple months, I noticed that he didn't want to see me as often as before. I should have took to heart the smirks his roommate would give me whenever I came by. You know, one of those "girl, if you only knew" looks.

Later, one of my friends asked me if my boyfriend and I were still kickin' it. When a friend asks a question like this, it usually means she knows something. I said we were. She hesitated and then told me that he was seen at the movies with another woman – a senior student. She didn't know if she recognized him right off because he did a great job of staying very low-key. She described his car pretty accurately since that was the only thing she had a solid description of since my first date with him. My friend told me what movie she saw the couple go into. We timed the movie and she gave me a ride back to the theater so I can see for myself. Sure enough, he was exiting the theater with a more mature-looking woman.

Now realize this. I was young and stupid. I wasn't wild, but I could get turned up pretty easily. I had my girls with me. I made a scene... When my boyfriend recognized me and perceived that I was a tad bit upset, he rushed his date out the door as quickly as possible. He ensured that she got into the car safely and basically sped off. My evening ended up with me in tears of rage, betrayal, and utter embarrassment. After he finally took one of my calls, I asked him why he didn't just tell me he was moving on. I would accept that better. He blurted out one of the lamest lines I ever heard. He said, "I thought we had an open relationship." What?! Where did he get that crap from?

It really didn't cross my mind that I was dating someone who would be graduating shortly after we'd met. What kind of life was I really expecting with this man anyway? I had three more years left in college and he was going to be soon gone to pursue a career. At the beginning of our relationship, I was very optimistic. I felt that he and I would be in love and eventually get married. I felt what we had was real and that our age difference was of no consequence because I was a mature young woman.

By choosing the right target, even socially awkward men can succeed at playing the game. I was the type of target that pretty much did all the work. I did it all in my own mind. I down-played myself by rushing in with the first guy that picked me over my lighter-skinned counterpart. I disrespected myself by not asking the right questions and setting a standard. I made a lot of mistakes simply because of ignorance and impatience. Remember, just because you are not the person playing the game, you must be aware that you can still be in one – someone else's...

<u>NOTES</u>

NOTES

GIVING UP THE GAME

CHAPTER 9

FRIENEMIES

When I was a little boy, I remember my dad telling me that I may think that everyone is my friend, but when I grow up, I'll be able to count my true friends on one hand. Basically, he was trying to tell me that everyone who I thought was my friend wasn't.

There's not many people that I know who haven't experienced betrayal. I want to share a story of betrayal I experienced at the hands of a person I thought was a real friend, a person I've known since I was in high school. People that run this type of game are only in the relationship to get something out of it. If your use becomes void, so does the so-called friendship.

These type of people I refer to as "frienemies." They are ever-present and if you are not watchful at all times, you can be susceptible to their deception and fickle ways. You could even suffer a setback or worse if you're not careful.

A "frienemy" can come in and steal your significant other, your idea, the money out of your bank account, even the gold teeth out of your mouth!

Without giving too many details, I want to tell you about such an incident I experienced a few years ago by the hands of someone whom I considered a true friend.

Around 2008, I had an inspired idea that I felt would help a lot of people and started on this project. This project required technical skills in certain areas that I didn't possess at the time. I knew I needed to pull in some help if this project would ever get off the ground.

I'll call this "frienemy" Joe. I met Joe in the new neighborhood my parents moved to when I got into high school. He had a reputation for being a cool guy, but also a bit sneaky. We became friends and hung out a lot. In the early 90's, I started a business and pulled him in on it. Joe was always very opinionated and we would sometimes lightly knock heads over simple things like the way I dressed. I used to wear shirt and ties a lot. He claimed that I needed to dress down more. I didn't agree totally because I feel that when you're doing business with people, you can't look like a thug from the street. He would also criticize my approach in certain business dealings. I adjusted some of the things he critiqued. I even changed up my dress some. Anytime I would disagree with him, there seemed to be a problem. Ironically, when I followed his advice, he would smile big and everything would be just fine. I began to notice something that signaled to me that I needed to be a little more watchful with him around my girlfriend at that time. I tried to put those suspicions away because he was my homeboy. Of course, I could trust him. He wouldn't do anything to betray my friendship.

We later partnered to create a product and had it in stores. A lot of people thought our product was great.

After that project, we sort of went our separate ways for a while. Money started getting tight and foolishly, I resorted back to crime. But this time, it was white-collar crime. I caught up with Joe and told him about my latest scheme. I involved him in the details of my plan along with a couple other accomplices. When the plan was implemented, we experienced success to the tune of almost $10,000 in my pocket. I left town afterwards.

Months passed by. One day, he convinced me to come back to Florida. He offered me his couch to crash with him for a while. I tried to go legit, but after a few months, I got that itch again for easy money. I blew most of my previous score on my girlfriend and her sister and rent. Next thing you know, we were back at white-collar crime again. But as fate would have it, we got jammed up and the cops had guns pointed at our heads. They separated us. I stuck to the prearranged script that had gotten us out of situations time and again. They still tried to press me to talk and give up my partner, but I wouldn't. I may have been a lot of things on the street, but I was never a snitch.

They left the room to go talk to Joe and after serval minutes, they came back smirking like they had everything they needed to know. One of them made a slight remark that further gave evidence to that. I wondered if that dude snitched on me. We were soon escorted to booking.

We got bonded out and a few of his friends were stepping to me as though I was the one who had snitched because they would never believe that Joe would ever do anything like that. To add insult to injury, I was blamed for getting him involved in the first place. I thought to myself, "Are you serious? This is a grown man who can make his own decisions. I didn't put a gun to his head to make him do anything."

I couldn't prove that he snitched, and although I was mad, I tried my best not to show it. Even if he did snitch, this is a natural consequence when you are involved in crime. I was quick to forgive in my heart because we were boys and no one is perfect. This was just how I chose to view the situation. I apologized to Joe for getting him into all of that mess and didn't hang too close to him after that.

Eventually, I lost contact with him. I would later go to prison for four years for the crimes I committed.

I eventually left the life of crime alone altogether. Even when times got hard, I kept my faith, believing that God would make a way somehow. Time and time again God has shown me that because I choose to put Him first, it is a big part of why He meets all of my needs.

Ever since I was a child, I was always free- hearted and generous. I always wanted to help others. When I grew up, I said that if I ever made it big, I would take the hood with me. Even when I was doing crime, I would take some of what I made and gave to homeless people and others in need. To Joe's credit, so did he.

I saw ministry as a way to give back. My wife and I joined a small church, but the people had big hearts. The pastor was excellent in everything he did and although the church was small in members, it had a big church feel to it. I was involved in street ministry - going out and encouraging people, telling them how I felt God had changed my life and that He could do the same for them if they gave Him a chance. I led children's church for a while because I love the youth. Then one day, God put a big idea in my heart.

GIVING UP THE GAME

Now that you have the background, it's time to bring it back current. This God-inspired idea is what prompted me to reach back out to Joe after all of those years. I learned from others that he went to college for the very thing I was trying to do. A mutual friend gave me his number. He, his crew, and I met and talked over coffee.

Joe advised me of the best way to approach the project. I gleaned a lot from him. I was always a fast learner, especially when it came to something I was interested in. The project was so much fun and it was something I thought I could do for the rest of my life. To me, this was it. I could get paid for helping people in this method.

Looking back, I understand that I should have formed an agreement with them for the project instead of trying to go into business with them. After all, so many years had passed. I had no idea the type of person Joe was at this point in his life. All I ran with was what he presented - a hard-working guy with a dream. I, of all people, should have known that nothing is what it seems to be all the time.

During the project, I began noticing some of the same things I saw in him when we were in partnership before. He was still very opinionated, but hey, there's nothing wrong with having an opinion, right?

GIVING UP THE GAME

We completed the project and were in planning stages of doing a few more. The initial project was the testing ground and we learned a lot from some of the mistakes we made. We decided that we were ready to do something on a grander scale. When we first started, we agreed that on each project, we would switch roles so that everyone would get experience in each role of the business. This would have been great if it had played out that way, but it didn't. I'll explain.

I went on to get into negotiations with a local business owner who had done very good business in Tampa. I've known him for years. This gentleman made big money as a real estate investor. He offered to support the project financially because he believed in me. I was also negotiating with a local business woman who had a successful cosmetic line. I lightly discussed these prospective projects with a few people and they all thought they were great projects.

I brought the idea back to the group and got no support. Actually, I was scrutinized to the hilt and Joe was at the helm. He acted like he didn't even want to meet with either of the prospects. I told them how and why I felt it would work, but nothing changed. One partner was neutral. The other one always supported Joe no matter what he did.

Satirically, when it was a project that Joe brought to the table, everyone was on board. I supported him for almost two years after my project was completed, but eventually lost interest because of the trend I started to see as to how the consensus always went in favor of Joe's ideas and no one else's. I took issue with one of the projects Joe took on for moral reasons. I'd come too far in how I lived my life to turn around and be involved with anything that could potentially act as a catalyst for me to go back to living a wild lifestyle. So I sent an email to him and the group and restated some of the things we initially stated that we were about as a team. I proposed that if we were currently at the point where we're doing sketchy projects, we should revisit our original intent when we formed the company. I invited the group to meet later in order to discuss. Joe got offended and went off! He accused me of hiding behind an email. Email was a common form of communication for me throughout our relationship. I find it helpful to flush out my thoughts without being interrupted.

Around that time, things where happening relationally and financially in my home and I had to focus my attention it. Finally, I met with the group and told them that I couldn't continue and that I needed to take a break for a while.

GIVING UP THE GAME

What happened next? Joe, in an angry tone, told me that he wished me well in life and there was no hard feelings (even though all of his mannerisms communicated the opposite.) The neutral partner tried explain that I wasn't saying that I didn't want to ever come back to be a part of what they were doing, but that I just needed a break to focus on my family's needs. Joe didn't listen, of course. He left that meeting angry. How did I know? He blocked me on Facebook (ha ha). A few years later, I learned from a mutual friend that Joe offered up that the reason the group broke up was because I wanted to make it all about me. Serious?

Okay. I know you may be asking what all of this has to do with game. I'll tell you. But first, I'll mention something I left out to draw out the suspense.

Shortly after forming the company, during a one-on-one conversation, Joe thanked me for contacting him with the opportunity of my project because he was about to give up on his dream. My project breathed new air back into him.

You see, many times people appear to be friends simply because they may want something from you. In other instances, people are friends to you as long as you are in the dependent position - needing them for something. Being needed gives many people a sense of power and superiority. In this case, Joe used my idea as a launching pad to fulfill his longtime dream. The project that I initiated brought him an award. He's since gone on to receive another for work he's done. I will admit that his work has gotten better over time. Congrats, Joe.

Looking back at our history, I reflect that as long as I needed his help whether it was a place to crash or helping me get money on the street or whenever I did what he told me or wanted me to do, he was cool with the relationship. When I tried to do things my own way or was in the lead, there was a problem.

In relationships, keep your heart open, but don't forget to keep your mind open as well. Sometimes we overlook things and are not rational when emotions are involved. While it is divine to overlook a transgression, it is stupid to be close to someone when they have proven that they are not for you.

Some things we can live with for sure, but a user isn't one of them. Using someone isn't always about money as I've just shown you. The game is always about domination and winning at another's expense.

GIVING UP THE GAME

In the book, *7 habits of Highly Effective People*, the late author talks a lot about win-win relationships where everything is done for a mutual benefit of all parties involved. He also mentioned how interdependent relationships are not like dependent ones where one person is always in need of the other. They are not like independent ones, where the attitude is that a person doesn't need anyone. Interdependent relationships are not codependent relationships where someone has lost the connection to his or her core self so that his or her thinking and behavior revolves around someone or something external.

Interdependent relationships speak to a community consciousness. A person or people with an interdependent attitude contributes greatly to their families, their communities and society because they realize that they have a special gift, talent or some kind of knowledge to bring to the table that will benefit all. These individuals are not afraid nor offended when someone else is prospering in some area or gets promotion. They help others succeed and are not afraid to call on others for help when they need it.

If you find yourself in the company of such beautiful souls, it's like a breath of fresh air. There are many talented, gifted and educated people in the world, but give me a person with the right attitude, and we can conquer the world. Crabs in the bucket are made for one thing, EATING! Let their venomous words, their mocking laughter at your dreams, their backstabbing actions be your food that causes you to excel. Don't get into the bucket with these crabs because you may never get out.

I've had other "frienemies" who have capitalized on information and ideas they've gotten from me. They even promoted it as their own original idea, never thinking once to give me credit for anything. So what. It's nice to be acknowledged, but I don't live for that. I just want to take care of my family and those that are truly down for me.

Never chase people. If they leave your life, it's for your good, believe me. You have to have thick skin and say to yourself that they look better going than coming. Lastly, forgive your enemies, recognize game, and keep it moving to higher ground.

GIVING UP THE GAME

NOTES

NOTES

CHAPTER 10

SURFING THE PEWS

What keeps many people from coming to Jesus and getting saved is the idea that the church is full of hypocrites. In response to this notion, I've heard several pastors reference the church as a hospital full of sick people coming to be healed. If a person isn't "healed" of his lust, pride, jealousy, etc., using the aforementioned analogy, then of course you'll see these character flaws pop up from time to time. The problem comes when well-meaning pastors tell their members that if they express any hurt they've experienced at the hands of another member, in essence, they are wrong and need to grow up. While I do agree that people need to be at a spiritual level where they have thick skin, overlooking offenses in a spirit of understanding, there are situations where offenses are egregious or too frequent. I've talked to people who were afraid to talk to their pastor about their feelings of offence because the church's culture seems to blame the victim for how they feel instead of addressing the offenders who really do the damage. This, in essence, hinders what the church is trying to accomplish. But because of wanting to stay in the good graces of their pastor and the rest of the congregants, they hide their wounds. This leads to a place where healing doesn't occur. It is certainly important help people overcome the proclivity to think that it's acceptable to hold on to hurts and remain bitter. However, there needs to be a balanced message so that everyone gets their fair share of the rod of correction. Smile.

We may have personally known women or have heard of women revealing that a pastor or some leader on the church tried to sleep with them. This is especially disturbing in the black community because we have already seen an absence of strong leadership in so many areas such as protecting, guiding and providing for our women and children. So when a woman goes to a "man of God" for spiritual guidance (something she may not have had in her home or community) and becomes a target of a minister's lust, it hurts us all.

The next story is from a friend of mine. It shares how she handled a predator amongst the pasture. She was strong and didn't use this hurtful experience to keep her from coming to God or the church.

WOLF IN SHEEP'S CLOTHING

I decided to visit my old church one day. It was a church I used to attend with my husband almost two years prior. One of the associate pastors of this church gave me a call and asked me to come back to get involved with the ministry once again. Now, as a divorced woman, I thought I'd go back and check it out since my ex was no longer attending there and also at that particular time, I still hadn't found another church to call home.

I attended the church service about a week before New Year's Eve and had a great time. The pastor invited me back for their New Year's Eve celebration. My life had been pretty dry and boring since my divorce. I stayed home a lot and had little interest in dating. I figured that attending a New Year's Eve celebration in the Lord's house was a way for me to get out and have a little fun.

It was New Year's Eve night and I had excitement in my heart as I approached the front door of the church with my five-year-old son in hand. We made our way in to find a seat. About 10 minutes later, a very attractive man came and sat next to us. He immediately complimented me on my shoes as he introduced himself as Michael while smiling and waving at my son. I replied with a kind thank you, but at the same time, I was trying to ignore him so I could keep my focus on the main purpose on why I was there. I was there to seek the Lord's direction as I ended an old year, embarking upon a new one.

As we sat waiting for the service to begin, I was able to detect that this man was well-known by everyone in the church. He was also a part of the head pastor's security team. On the other side of me, a dear friend named Tracey sat. When I first started attending this church some years prior as a married woman, Tracy was one of the primary people that I became close with. Tracey knew what I had been through with my marriage/divorce. As we sat there talking for a while, she said that she was proud to see that I had bounced back. She then turned and told me that God was getting ready to bless me. Smiling, I received what she said because in my heart I believed it to be true.

Later that evening, Tracey quietly slipped me a note saying that she had personally known Michael, the man on the other side of me, for many years having the opportunity to work with him through the ministry. She spoke highly of his character. It was then that I realized that I was being set up. Was this what she was speaking of when she spoke of a blessing? It turned out that Michael had observed me the prior week I'd visited and saw me talking with Tracey. Through this, he began to inquire of me by asking Tracey all sorts of questions concerning my life. I understood the picture. Realizing that I was sandwiched in between the two of them, I was still determined to stay focused.

At some point during the service, Michael wrote the word "confidence" in the notepad of his phone in all caps and showed it to me. Puzzled, I asked him what it meant. He explained that from the moment he saw me the week prior, he wanted to approach me but didn't have the nerve. He said that the Lord spoke to his heart and told him to have confidence about meeting me. However, when he looked around for me after that service, I was already gone. Michael looked me in my eyes and stated, "This time I'm not letting you get away from me again." He then confessed that this was the reason he was sitting next to me. I took a deep breath as I did not know what to say in response. I just smiled, went within and began to ask the Lord what in the world was going on?!

When it came time for the church offering, Michael pulled out his check book and wrote a check for $250.00. Showing this check to me, he said, "I am sowing this seed for us." I said to myself that this dude is serious. No doubt he made it hard for me to stay focused as I began to wonder more about him. Tracey vouched that Michael was not only the greatest and best-looking catch in the entire church, but was also the most eligible one.

All throughout the rest of the night, Michael was the most perfect gentleman and beyond sweet. I found myself interested to know more, but still hesitant with my guards up not wanting to go into another relationship unless I knew it was God leading me.

It came time for the countdown to the New Year. As the entire church counted backwards 5, 4, 3, 2..., I looked over to notice Michael was reaching out for a New Year's Day hug. I gave him a quick hug, hugged Tracey, and stepped out into the walkway to hug others. We were all overjoyed to be celebrating the daybreak of a new year. New beginnings were in the air.

I knew Michael was waiting for me to come back to the area where he was standing. I finally decided to go back to my seat to grab my things and leave. Sure enough, he was waiting. My son had fallen asleep so I was reaching to pick him up. Before I could do so, Michael swooped him up instead. Seeing him holding my son in his arms as if the child belonged to him, I was touched. Michael then asked if he could walk me to my car. I agreed.

He gently laid my son down in the back seat of my vehicle and then asked if he could see me again. We stood there talking for a bit and then we exchanged phone numbers.

My home was about thirty-five minutes away. Michael immediately called as soon as I got on the road. We ended up talking until four o'clock that morning. He told me many things about himself. Towards the end of our conversation, he told me that he had everything he ever wanted in life except for marriage. He said he wanted to pursue me for marriage.

We met up at a nice restaurant for our first date and talked the night away. We were both very excited and nervous to be in each other's presence that we didn't even order food from the menu. It seemed unreal and was definitely highly euphoric, beyond any I'd ever experienced before. A waitress from another section walked by and told us that we looked so good together and took our picture. They say that a picture is worth a thousand words. This one was worth a million.

It had only been days, but each day of knowing Michael was breathtaking. One morning, he called explaining how he'd been up early praying. He said that the Lord spoke to him and that he had wrote down what was told to him by the Lord. He asked if he could proceed reading it to me. I agreed. Michael began to cry as he read unforgettable words spoken to him from the Lord about me and his position in my life as a protector, provider and a husband. We cried together. Now, my walls were completely torn down. I proceeded on in the relationship unguarded. I placed my heart in his hands.

About a good week into our relationship, he took me to his home and showed me each room inside. It was a very large four-bedroom house. He had been single for 12 years and was living there by himself. As we walked around from room to room, he looked at me and said, "I always wondered why I purchased this big house. I thought it was just because I liked the floor plan so much, but now I realize that I purchased it for you and your kids... who are now my kids." With that, he handed me the key to the front door. He also sat me down and gave me a card to open. As I opened it, a credit card fell out of it. He told me to use it whenever I needed gas, groceries, help paying a bill, etc.

Every day with him was literally like a dream come true. I thought to myself that my knight in shining amour had finally come for me. I would find myself weeping over the incredible joy he brought into my life. I thought that I could finally relax because now I was in the arms of safety. I found myself breathing again, exhaling. My smile wouldn't go away- it looked like it was plastered on my face!

A month had gone by and the dream was still alive. On this one particular day, I decided to sign onto Facebook. As I was scrolling down my newsfeed, suddenly I saw that a picture of me made onto the cover photo of Michael's profile page. Now everyone knew that we were an item. My ex and I had been apart for almost two years, but I still wondered how this was going to go over with everyone.

As time went on, Sunday after Sunday, I noticed that the women of the church were boldly staring at me and looking disturbed about the fact that I came in out of nowhere and snatched up the most attractive man inside the church. One woman told Michael not to get serious with me because I had four kids. Another woman, who didn't even know me, sent him a long text saying that I was a gold digger and that he shouldn't have any kids with me or I will keep him in court trying to get more money from him. She went on and on saying horrible things about me. It was apparent that many women in the church (even some of the married ones who also had crushes on him) were deeply bothered by our new-found relationship. They instantaneously started attacking it. I was literally shocked by their behavior and lies. More than anything, I was just plain hurt that church people would treat me in such a way.

We ignored them as best as we could, but I could tell he was also bothered because his reputation and his status were important to him. Shortly thereafter, Michael took my picture down as his Facebook cover. It was odd to me because he didn't even tell me he was going to take it down. I just stumbled across the fact that it was done. I just figured he wanted people to cool down with all the talk so taking the picture down was a means to do that. Of course, that was the exact excuse he gave for wanting to take it down.

One day, out of frustration to the backlash of our relationship, Michael wanted sexually intimacy for comfort. Although I wanted to be with him on that level, I quickly reminded him that there could be no sex before marriage because of my commitment to God and the mere fact that he said he would honor that from the beginning. Because I am yielding to the call of God on my life, there are certain things I just could not do. And at this point in my life, it is more important to me that I am in God's will for my life as opposed to being in a place that I am not supposed to be! Michael became even more frustrated, but now his frustration was with me. He insisted that we must have a "normal" relationship or it wasn't going to work. Tears rolled down my face as I realized he was threatening to take his love back if I couldn't give him what he wanted. Immediately, something changed. I could see it right before me. He had changed.

Soon thereafter, only days later, he became harsh and impatient when he would speak to me over the phone or in person. He was treating me in ways that communicated, "If you don't want to give me what I need, someone else will." Overnight, he was a completely different man than the one I'd originally met – the one I allowed myself to fall in love with. I was devastated by his new behavior. I wanted to give in to what he wanted just so I could keep the relationship going.

I cried out to God. I was crushed. I couldn't believe that I placed my heart into the wrong hands again and now it was broken into pieces. Before we were even over, Facebook revealed that he was already seeing someone else. Over the following three months, I found myself depressed, wondering if Michael would come back and fix things between us. I thought surly he would. After all the God that he talked to me about, surly he will do the right thing and live up to all the promises he made to me.

Michael never came back.

Hindsight is always 20/20. Looking back, I can clearly see the vital things that I overlooked because I was so caught up in his ability to speak and say all of the right things. Clearly, I moved utterly fast by giving my heart away too soon. Looking back, I see now how in subtle ways, he isolated me from the pastor that invited me to come back to that church. I see now that he did that to prevent me from having sound wisdom speaking in my ear - to prevent me from having an extra set of eyes that would see what I could not.

I learned not to be moved by what a person says, even if they say they come in the name of Jesus. It is important to watch their life for a while. The bible says that you will know a person by the fruit that they produce. Had I taken the time to inspect the fruit, I could have avoided the pain of that heartache. But at the same time, I realize that we serve a sovereign God and whatever happens in life has already passed through His hands. If God allowed it to come to my doorstep, then He can use it to process me and build me into His design for my life, which is my ultimate goal anyway!

The things that we go through may not be God-sent, but it can always be God-used if we don't get bitter and unforgiving, but instead embrace the choices we make by becoming accountable for our own actions. Looking within to seek to understand why we chose and how we chose in making the wrong decisions to connect with something or someone, teaches us how to move beyond making that same mistake in our future. It causes us to mature on a greater level.

Today, I am grateful that the heartbreak came earlier rather than later. I am glad that I severed all ties with Michael and moved on with my life. My experience with Michael taught me how to choose wiser and smarter. This experience has been used to help me bless and strengthen others. Because I know the power in Genesis 50:20 which states, "Yes, yes the enemy meant to destroy you with the adversities and calamities of life, BUT GOD will completely turn around what the enemy tried to annihilate you with and cause you to not only live, but also cause others to find life through you!" God saves us so that we will help to save others. Hallelujah!

<u>NOTES</u>

<u>NOTES</u>

CHAPTER 11

PORN: GAME OF SELF-DECEPTION

You're on a slippery slope when you mess around with pornography. Let me tell you a story of this one young woman who lived in my old neighborhood, Nuccio. I was in my early 20's and she was in her late 20's. I met her either in our apartment complex or at the 711 convenience store right in front of our complex. It's a well-known fact that guys are visual. Back then, I was only concerned with looks. Substance was a non-issue, especially since I didn't have much myself at the time. When I got this particular young lady's phone number, I felt like a pimp. The only problem was that my girlfriend and I lived together. One day, the young lady invited me over and I slipped away to her apartment. She offered me something to drink. I said I'll take a water. Boy was I nervous, I ain't gonna lie.

She said that she had to go take care of something in the back room. She popped in a VCR tape and told me to watch the movie until she came back.

Man, I was blowed! I saw people doing all kinds of things with and to each other. She set me up. It wasn't long before I was all hot and bothered.

After about 20 minutes, she came back with very little conversation and escorted me to her bedroom. I left her house feeling giddy, thinking that I came up big time especially since I didn't have too much game back then. We engaged liked this several times before she moved away. She left behind a persistent parting gift – I was totally hooked on porn.

I deceived myself into believing that watching porn enhanced couples' love life. How else was a brother going to learn all of those new sexual positions? From high school to college, teachers and counselors are telling students that this is normal and acceptable behavior. I even had a close friend tell me that in one of their health classes, their college professor encouraged them to "explore" themselves because masturbation is healthy. I came to find out later that watching pornography actually robs a relationship.

Even with all of the self-justifications, I always felt that there was something not quite right about it, especially since I grew up in the church. But today as I write this book, I am free from that addiction. I tried for years to get rid of this secret sin that I was too embarrassed to talk about to anyone. Then I came across a British study that explained how pornography is literally as addictive as drugs. The study finds that addiction to pornography leads to similar brain activity patterns found in alcohol and drug addicts.

Researchers from Cambridge University found that MRI scans of 19 addictive pornography users showed that the reward centers of the brain reacted to explicit images in a similar way that an alcoholic might respond to liquor or beer advertisements. When an alcoholic sees an ad for a drink, their brain will light up in a certain way and they will be stimulated in a certain way. Researchers are seeing this same kind of activity in users of pornography.

Porn also creates a neurochemical imbalance and causes you to focus on multiple images, body types, partners and scenarios. In the process, the focus on one's spouse is lost.

Dr. Norman Doidge, author of *The Brain That Changes Itself: Stories of Personal Triumph from the Frontiers of Brain Science* explains that "human beings exhibit an extraordinary degree of sexual plasticity compared with other creatures." What he means by "plasticity" is that our sexuality and our brains are molded by our experiences, interactions, and other means of learning which is why people vary in what they say is attractive or what turns them on. The brain actually creates neural pathways that label a specific type of person or activity as arousing. The reason pornography use is so addictive is because the brain releases a flood of hormonal and neurochemical rewards. This causes the brain to map out neural pathways for pornography use quickly.

Gary Wilson and Anthony Jack in the book *Your Brain on Porn*, reviews a study showing that when women and men were exposed to porn, they were less pleased with their partner's sexual performance, physical appearance and affection. Pornography users always come to a point where they compare their significant other with the images in adult videos.

Many couples use pornography to "spice up their relationship," but some take it a step further...

CONSENSUAL NON-MONOGAMY

Some years ago, I was doing signage work for a local business with an old friend. This guy was real cool and a shrewd business man. We made some good money together. My wife and I visited him a couple of times to talk about business unrelated to what he and I were into. One evening, after a long day of prospecting and dealing with customers, he approached me with a proposition. I'll call him Tony.

Tony let me into his private world of freaktopia. He told me that he liked the way me and my wife carried ourselves and because he's a private person, he didn't normally share this information with just anybody. I forgot exactly how he put it, but essentially, he invited my wife and me for a night of swapping.

I was shocked to say the least. I wondered what made him get that comfortable with me. My wife and I never (and never will) dabble in that stuff. I responded gently that we couldn't and wouldn't participate because of our faith. I did my best to come across in a way that didn't come off offensive or like I thought that I was better than him. He understood and we never discussed the matter anymore.

I am a straight novice to swapping. When doing research for this book, I asked Tony for information concerning the swinging lifestyle and how swingers seduce couples into this world. I found out that there were rules to the swapping game. In conversation, he told me that swapping couples are more honest than straight couples. I was like, "Huh?" Tony said (in his fatalistic view) that within most heterosexual couples, one or both of the partners eventually cheat or at least have a secret desire to be with someone else.

Swappers are open and honest about their feelings and embrace them. They agree to have sex with other consenting couples, but at the end of the day, they go home to their own partner. I don't know what to call this - maybe a committed open relationship? I know that's an oxymoron, but that's the best way I can describe this type of relationship.

Folks, sex is not equivalent to intimacy. Swinging relationships give people the excitement of sex without the intimacy of a committed monogamous relationship. It's unfortunate that many people choose to deceive themselves into believing that they need these extra relationships to make their marriages better instead of investing the hard work it takes to make a marriage work. After all, on their wedding day, couples see their future spouse as being worth spending the rest of their life with for better or for worse. It seems that many people marry for the better only and lie to the priest or pastor about being committed when things aren't so rosy. If you'll lie to the person of God, you'll most likely cheat, swap, indulge in porn, etc. Remember to self-evaluate so you don't self-destruct.

<u>NOTES</u>

NOTES

CHAPTER 12

MILKING THE COW

The old saying still stands firm, "Why buy the cow, when the milk is free?" Why doesn't anyone listen to this wisdom from our ancestors? Cohabitating or "shacking up" has produced too many baby mamas and baby daddies. Children produced in these situations grow up with all kinds of problems.

Research shows that cohabiting dissolves families, impacts children negatively, and increases instances of sexual abuse, drug abuse, crime, illiteracy, and out-of-wedlock pregnancies. In addition, studies reveal that only 45 percent of couples who live together go on to marry. Of those who do marry, there is a 45 percent higher risk for divorce than people who have never cohabitated. Only 15 out of every 100 shack-ups will result in a "long-term, successful marriage."

It's not just the guys these days. Women seem to be afraid of commitment too and prefer celebrating their anniversaries of being a couple. So many people are content with playing house as opposed to loving themselves enough not to allow their precious years to go by with a lover who won't make a commitment to them. Also, how can you expect your family to accept someone as "family" when you're not even willing to officially make them family?

Splitting the rent to save for marriage and living with someone to see if you are compatible sound like good ideas, but they are not.

THE MARRIAGE DILEMMA

I have taken the liberty to include information concerning the effects of premarital sex and cohabitation on overall quality of life and long-term relationships.

- Those who live together before marriage are the least likely to marry each other. About 40 percent of cohabiting unions in the United States break up without the couple getting married. One of the reasons may be that those who cohabitate drift from one partner to another in search of the 'right' person. The average cohabitant has several partners in a lifetime.

- Those who live together before marriage have higher separation and divorce rates. *Psychology Today* reported the findings of Yale University sociologist Neil Bennett that cohabiting women were 80 percent more likely to separate or divorce than were women who had not lived with their spouses before marriage. It was determined that living in a non-marital union "has a direct negative impact on subsequent marital stability," perhaps because living in such a union "undermines the legitimacy of formal marriage" and so "reduces commitment of marriage."

- Those who live together before marriage have unhappier marriages. A study by the National Council on Family Relations of 309 newlyweds found that those who cohabited first were less happy in marriage.

- Those who have had premarital sex are more likely to have extramarital affairs as well. Premarital sexual attitudes and behavior do not change after one marries. If a woman lives with a man before marriage, she is more likely to cheat on him after marriage. Research indicates that if one is willing to experience sex before marriage, a higher level of probability exists that one will do the same afterwards. This is especially true for women. Those who engaged in sex before marriage are more than twice as likely to have extramarital affairs as those who did not have premarital sex. When it comes to staying faithful, married partners have higher rates of loyalty every time.

- Those who have "trial run" marriages do not have better marriages. Research indicates that couples who live together before marriage have significantly lower marital satisfaction than those who do not cohabit and they have weaker marriages, not stronger ones.

- Those who live together have no lasting commitments or responsibilities. Cohabitation involves no public commitment, no pledge for the future, no official pronouncement of love and responsibility. Theirs is essentially a private arrangement based on an emotional bond. The 'commitment' of living together is simply a month-to-month rental agreement that implies, "As long as you behave yourself and keep me happy, I'll stick around." Marriage, on the other hand, is much more than a love partnership. It is a public event that involves legal and societal responsibilities. It brings together not just two people but also two families and two communities. It is not just for the here and now; it is, most newlyweds hope, 'till death do us part.' Getting married changes what you expect from your mate and yourself.

- Those who live together miss something in the maturing process. In this "alternative lifestyle," the aim is to have all the benefits and privileges of a mature, married person without accepting the responsibilities which maturity demands. Cohabitation also points to a missing ingredient in the process of becoming mature: the willingness to make commitments and live up to them. A willingness to defer immediate pleasures in pursuit of a worthwhile goal is a mark of maturity.

- Those living together avoid dealing with some of the joint decisions that married couples have to make. For example, money and property tend to be either 'his' or 'hers', not 'ours.' Consequently, it isn't all that important how he or she spends his or her money. In-laws are rarely a factor. They often disapprove and stay aloof from the couple (Dunagan 1993).

- Those having premarital sex may be fooled into marrying a person who is not right for them. Sex can emotionally blind. Real love can stand the test of time without the support of physical intimacy. If you establish a mutually satisfying sexual relationship, you lose objectivity and actually cheat on the test of time. The only way to rationally decide whether your love is for keeps is to remove any preoccupation with Eros, sexual love. Otherwise, you may marry a mirage, not a person you really know.

- Those living together have superficial and significantly weaker relationships. Researchers have found that couples who live together before marriage have weaker marriages (DeMars and Leslie 1984).

- Those who live together have more difficulty resolving conflicts. A recent study at Penn State University (Brown & Booth 1997) comparing the relationship qualities of 682 cohabiters and 6,881 married couples (both White and Black, aged 19 to 48 years of age), found that cohabiters argue, shout and hit more than married couples.

- Those who live together before marriage often lay a foundation of distrust and lack of respect. Premarital sex lays the groundwork for comparisons, suspicions, and mistrust. Real trust grows in the context of the life-long commitment within a monogamous relationship of marriage.

- Those who live together do not experience the <u>best sex</u>. The best sex is found in the marriage relationship. It is reported that if a couple abstains from sex before marriage, they are 29 to 47 percent more likely to enjoy sex afterward. In a study by Dr. Evelyn Duvall and Dr. Judson Landis, evidence was found that premarital sex was not as satisfying.

Don't settle for less when you can have the best!!!

<u>NOTES</u>

CHAPTER 13

CHEATING: AN ACT OF VIOLENCE

While writing this book, it came to me that this piece wouldn't be complete without discussing violence. When I think about violence, I think about the acts of hitting, cutting and other physically hurtful acts and hurtful outbursts. Many people would never think of cheating on their spouse or significant other as an act of violence. Hurtful if the other finds out, but not violence. We also, hardly if ever, wouldn't think of violence as game, but it is. It is a form of manipulation and controlling another person. Remember, game is about getting what you want, making the victim submissive in order to maintain control.

An article in Australia's *The Age* details how infidelity and abuse are one in the same.

Why is infidelity abusive? Why is it sometimes a form of psychological and emotional violence? Because infidelity can be as devastating as a violent physical attack. It results in humiliation, hurt and loss for the injured partner. The betrayal is usually perceived as a direct attack on the faithful partner's worth as a person and as a partner.

GIVING UP THE GAME

One of the methods pimps use (and many men in general) is to break a woman's spirit like a man breaks a wild horse. Once broken, they can rebuild the woman back up the way they want them. Any self-worth the woman has after that point is the one the pimp/man wants them to have. After the breaking, the woman's self-worth is wrapped up in the thought of how good she is at pleasing her pimp/man and being all he wants her to be.

Growing up listening to all of the misogynistic music by artists like Too Short and most of the Miami based rap music, me, my friends, and other guys I knew had a distrust and hatred for women and thought that it was our job to punish them for being whores and skanks by nature. It didn't matter if they were the classy, hard-working, the nine-to-five type, the quiet girl in college, the church girl, or the club-hopping hoochie, they all had the same nature and you couldn't trust any of them.

This brick wall that we put up around our hearts kept us from looking at women as human beings, fallible like we all were. We never saw that they were special and unique in their own right. The truth of the matter is that they were all the same. Many young women are just like men in the sense that they are just trying to find their way in life and sometimes make mistakes along the way.

GIVING UP THE GAME

Our mindset kept us from really living and enjoying our lives in relationships. Many of my friends who are now in their middle ages are still not married because of this flawed mentality that keeps them stuck in a mode of constant conquest - going from one one-night stand and temporary relationship to the next. They can never settle down with just one person because they never learned to trust anyone.

This mentality always causes those given over to it to see the worst in people. This eventually leads a person to physical violence. Neurologists estimate that a person is aware of about 2,000 bits of information per minute. As impressive as this sounds, our brain is actually processing 400 billion bits of information per minute. If your frame of reference is negative in any area, your mind will only process information that verifies your negative or flawed belief in that area.

When a person has had a sexual experience with any of the women aforementioned, this was "proof" that all women were whores and freaks.

As fate would have it, I ended up having a daughter while I was in the idiot phase of my youth. My first daughter is such a blessing. Some days, though, I lament that I wasn't more mature for her when she made her glorious entrance into my life. I now have three daughters in total. As a proud father, of course you know I definitely had to rethink my philosophy concerning women. There is no way my little precious girls would ever be considered a whore or freak. It takes time to unlearn foolishness just like it takes time to create a healthy habit or thought pattern. Having daughters caused an instant paradigm shift.

When I married my wife, this was a huge feat for me! This meant that I trusted her more than any other woman. I trusted her with my heart. But after marriage, my old instincts kicked in on several occasions. The slightest thing like her not answering my phone call would have me going nuts. I would come at her like, "I called you at two o'clock and you didn't call me back. What's up with that?!"

I thank God that I have matured over the years. Having been involved with so many women who had significant others (women you wouldn't expect would ever cheat on their man) left me scared and afraid that this would come back on me. All of these experiences haunted me and was a constant reminder on how not to treat people. Almost everyone I know loves sex. I had to learn not to look at women as sex machines, but as human beings, as equals.

Take a few moments to look at the following diagrams of the wheel of control and violence.

GIVING UP THE GAME

Power and Control Wheel courtesy of maplegate.info

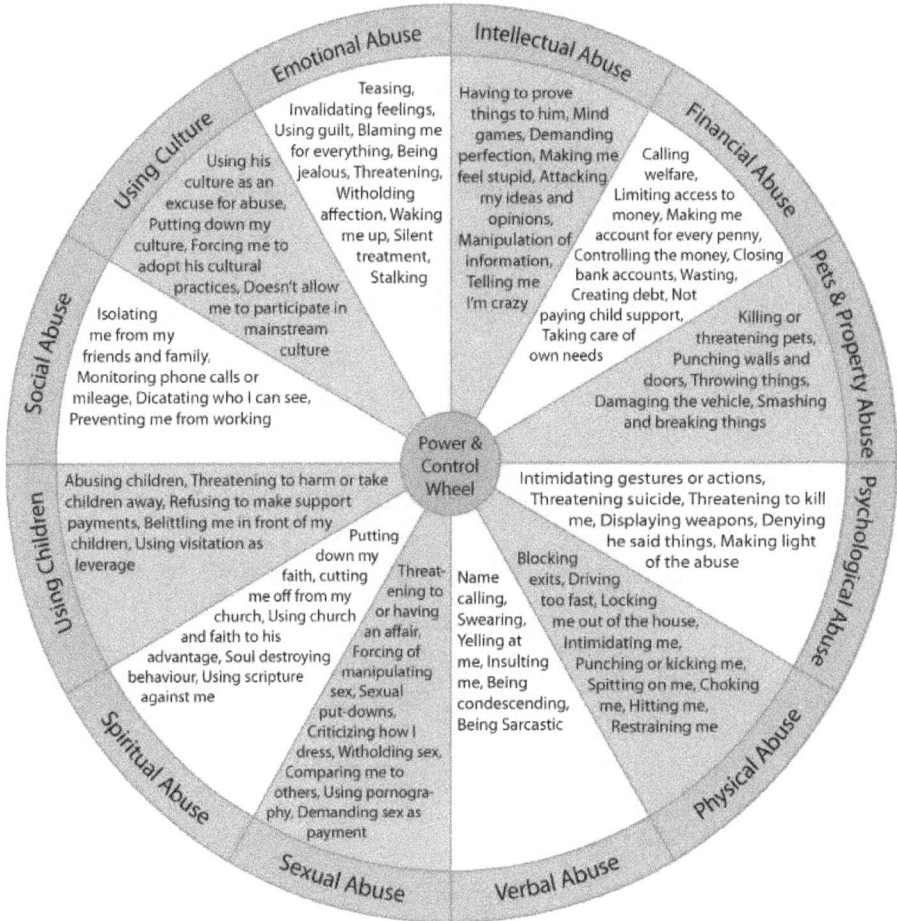

Emotional Abuse
Teasing, Invalidating feelings, Using guilt, Blaming me for everything, Being jealous, Threatening, Witholding affection, Waking me up, Silent treatment, Stalking

Intellectual Abuse
Having to prove things to him, Mind games, Demanding perfection, Making me feel stupid, Attacking my ideas and opinions, Manipulation of information, Telling me I'm crazy

Using Culture
Using his culture as an excuse for abuse, Putting down my culture, Forcing me to adopt his cultural practices, Doesn't allow me to participate in mainstream culture

Financial Abuse
Calling welfare, Limiting access to money, Making me account for every penny, Controlling the money, Closing bank accounts, Wasting, Creating debt, Not paying child support, Taking care of own needs

Social Abuse
Isolating me from my friends and family, Monitoring phone calls or mileage, Dicatating who I can see, Preventing me from working

Pets & Property Abuse
Killing or threatening pets, Punching walls and doors, Throwing things, Damaging the vehicle, Smashing and breaking things

Power & Control Wheel

Using Children
Abusing children, Threatening to harm or take children away, Refusing to make support payments, Belittling me in front of my children, Using visitation as leverage

Psychological Abuse
Intimidating gestures or actions, Threatening suicide, Threatening to kill me, Displaying weapons, Denying he said things, Making light of the abuse

Spiritual Abuse
Putting down my faith, cutting me off from my church, Using church and faith to his advantage, Soul destroying behaviour, Using scripture against me

Sexual Abuse
Threatening to or having an affair, Forcing of manipulating sex, Sexual put-downs, Criticizing how I dress, Witholding sex, Comparing me to others, Using pornography, Demanding sex as payment

Verbal Abuse
Name calling, Swearing, Yelling at me, Being condescending, Being Sarcastic, Blocking exits, Driving too fast, Locking me out of the house, Intimidating me, Punching or kicking me, Spitting on me, Choking me, Hitting me, Restraining me

Physical Abuse

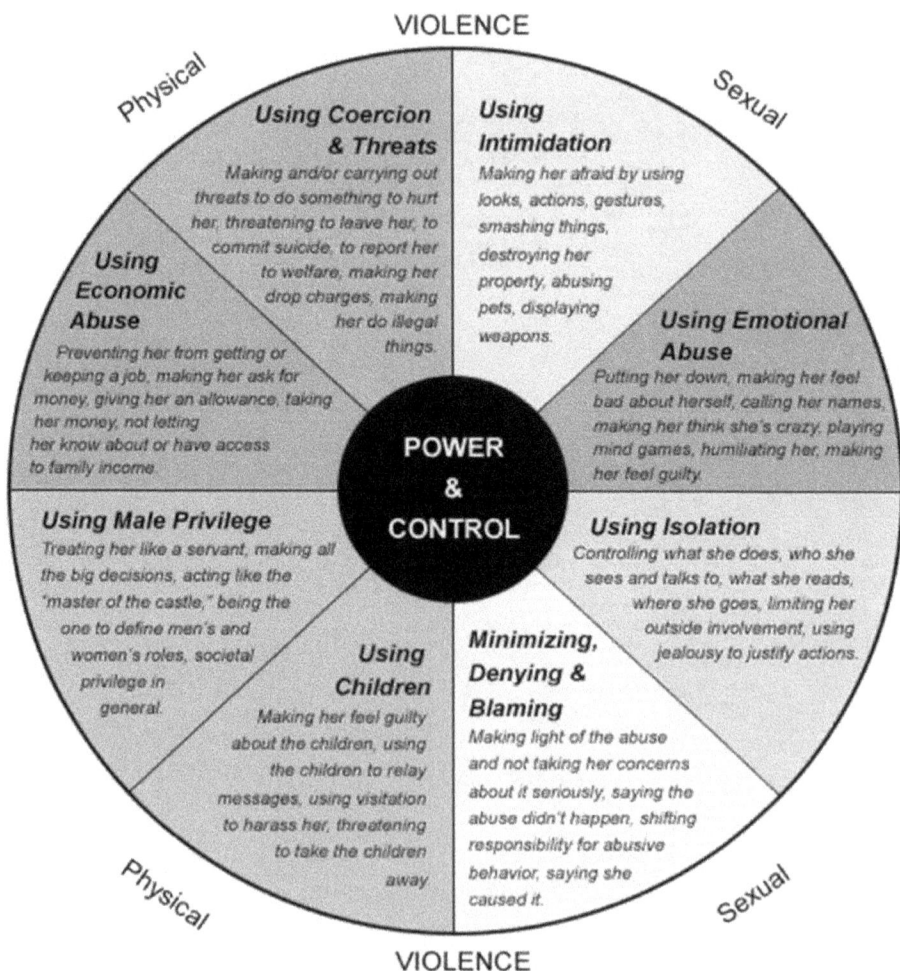

VIOLENCE

Physical   Sexual

Using Coercion & Threats
Making and/or carrying out threats to do something to hurt her, threatening to leave her, to commit suicide, to report her to welfare, making her drop charges, making her do illegal things.

Using Intimidation
Making her afraid by using looks, actions, gestures, smashing things, destroying her property, abusing pets, displaying weapons.

Using Economic Abuse
Preventing her from getting or keeping a job, making her ask for money, giving her an allowance, taking her money, not letting her know about or have access to family income.

Using Emotional Abuse
Putting her down, making her feel bad about herself, calling her names, making her think she's crazy, playing mind games, humiliating her, making her feel guilty.

POWER & CONTROL

Using Male Privilege
Treating her like a servant, making all the big decisions, acting like the "master of the castle," being the one to define men's and women's roles, societal privilege in general.

Using Isolation
Controlling what she does, who she sees and talks to, what she reads, where she goes, limiting her outside involvement, using jealousy to justify actions.

Using Children
Making her feel guilty about the children, using the children to relay messages, using visitation to harass her, threatening to take the children away

Minimizing, Denying & Blaming
Making light of the abuse and not taking her concerns about it seriously, saying the abuse didn't happen, shifting responsibility for abusive behavior, saying she caused it.

Physical   Sexual

VIOLENCE

GIVING UP THE GAME

HONEYMOON
Victims Response:
- sets up counseling for him
- drops legal proceedings
- agrees to return, stay or take him back
- forgives
- hopeful
- relieved
- happy

Abuser:
- apologizes
- promises won't happen again • tries to justify his behavior
- blames drugs or alcohol
- declares love • wants to be intimate • buys gifts • promises to get help • promises to go to church
- enlists family support • cries
- threatens suicide

DENIAL

Abuser:
- sensitive
- nitpicks • yelling
- withholds affection
- putdowns • threatens
- crazy making behavior
- destroys property
- accusations of unfaithfulness
- isolates her
- engaging her to argue

Abuser: verbally abuses & humiliates • slap • punch • kick • choke • grab • forces sex • beats • prevents her from calling police or leaving • harasses & abuses children • restrains • spits • stalks • use of weapons • objects thrown

TENSION BUILDING
Victims Response:
- attempts to calm
- tries to reason
- tries to satisfy with food
- agrees with
- avoidance
- withdraws
- compliant
- nurtures

ACUTE EXPLOSION
Victims Response:
- protects self any way
- tries to reason & calm
- may or may not call police
- leaves • fights back

131

There are common characteristics between victims of physical abuse and victims of infidelity:

- Both can become an ongoing aspect of the relationship. Often, you'll see a recurring cycle in which the abusive or cheating partner is repentant and the relationship functions well. Then another episode of abuse or infidelity will return.

- One partner may show short periods of remorse or guilt, but normally may seem insensitive to the pain that they have caused. Many will not accept responsibility for the suffering they've caused.

- The victim suffers from a lack of control over their life, low self-esteem, a sense of worthlessness, a dependency on their significant other, and a distorted sense of reality in which they may believe that what happens is their fault.

I was physically and emotionally abusive in my first two serious relationships. I made amends with those women and again apologize to them in this writing and to all women who have experienced acts of violence of any kind. I, as a man, have experienced emotional violence at the hands of a few women. I want to say that I forgive you. I hope that men and women everywhere who read this book will realize that abuse of any kind should never be tolerated. We have to love ourselves more than to allow ourselves to receive the type of treatment that would tear down our sense of self-worth and self-respect.

If you don't have the wherewithal to truly love, then you should remain single rather than take another human being through hell. Everyone I know of was born of a woman. The mere fact that you are living and breathing is due in part to that fact.

I'm hard on the men because we are supposed to be the providers and protectors of women, not predators, regardless of what women do to us. And for the women who abuse men, don't complain when you reap what you sow and attract a dog in your life. You may call it soiling your wild oats as the old folks used to say, but what you're really doing is sowing death and destruction into your life and relationships.

GIVING UP THE GAME

<u>NOTES</u>

CHAPTER 14

GIVING UP THE GAME

People, beware! Once you give up your player card, you can never get it back nor should you want to. I have to tell you the story about 'Slick Nik'. Nikki (my wife) really wasn't slick at all. She was (and is) her genuine self with no fillers. I met this wonderful woman in Gainesville, FL right before she graduated from college. This girl was cooler than a fan. Man, this girl was (and still is) gorgeous! My preference of women as far as physical qualities were concerned was light-skinned black or Latino women with giant butts. Nikki broke the mold. She was of a darker complexion and had the shape of a supermodel. She was everything a man could want; beauty, brains, spirituality, and had a great sense of humor. I forgot to mention that she was great at playing the game of ...Spades. That's how we initially connected. She was everything I was consistently praying for in a woman for a couple of years before we met. Neither of us looked at the other for a love interest when we were hanging out, though. She was one of my "down" chicks, more like a little sister to me. She was 21 and I was 30. We both had age limits for the people we were willing to date. I didn't want to go five years above or below my current age. The funny thing is that this was one of her criteria as well. We both had our written lists of qualities we wanted to see in a significant other. We met at a time in my life when I was tired of the game and saw that it was a huge waste of time. I began to cut people off - places and things that were hindering me from becoming all that I knew God wanted me to be. In fact, I met Nikki only because we were attending the same church at the time. Nikki was surprisingly mature for her age and other women far older than her, whether a friend or acquaintance, were shocked when they discovered she was not their same age. She was, and still is, a great conversationalist. We would talk for hours on the phone and I would never get tired of listening to her. She held my attention in so many different ways. That was surprising to me because when it came to women, I had Attention Deficit Hyperactivity Disorder (ADHD). I couldn't focus on just one!

We were so close that people thought we were seeing each other, but that wasn't the case. The more I hung around her, the more I had to suppress the feelings that where bubbling up inside of me for her. I wanted to keep her strictly as a friend. All of my female friends before her I tried or did sleep with and I didn't want this to be another one of those good relationships that went bad.

I hated to see her hurt. She didn't know much about the games that men played. I started thinking that if she was with me, she would not have to go through the nonsense from those who just wanted to have fun with the ladies.

I moved back to Tampa thinking that I would never see her again because she was planning on moving to another state when she graduated. Things didn't work out the way she expected and ended up moving back to Tampa as well. She called me one day and we were back hanging out again.

One of my friends helped me to realize that I needed to stop trying to suppress the romantic feelings I had for Nikki. I wrestled with this for some time. Soon thereafter, I overheard her explaining how she prefers men to be forthright with how they felt. I took this as my queue to reveal my feelings to her. I knew she was a keeper and she meant business.

In the car at a McDonald's, I revealed my heart to her. She looked at me, smiled, and said that she didn't like me in that way. She added that if it was too uncomfortable to be around her knowing that she didn't want to have that type of relationship, to let her know and she would understand. Nikki was no joke, people. I played it cool and asked her to keep me in mind. Maybe she would change your mind later or maybe not. I just wanted to get it off of my chest.

No guy likes rejection, but I was glad I got it out. I had to force myself to get back to friend-mode with her. It didn't work, people. I was able to brush things off when I was out there in player- mode. I was able to shut my emotions off easily. But for some strange reason, I couldn't do this with Nikki. So I refused to give up. I had to work harder for her than I had to with any woman.

One night while I was working a late shift, I called Nikki to ask her to just give me a chance to love her. She started crying because at that exact time, a guy she opened up to and was trying to build a relationship with had let her down. She quickly ended the conversation with me to grieve. Nikki was very selective when it came to who she would date. Though she was very popular in college, she wasn't the type to give up sex so easy. So instead of seeing her for the great woman she was, most dudes would settle for the easy and go elsewhere to get their "needs" met.

I had to give her the game, the game her guy friends wouldn't because they didn't want to look bad in her eyes. She used to ask them questions, but they wouldn't tell her how guys really thought. They never divulged the things they did. Like me, they wanted to protect her, however, they wouldn't give her the game.

I wanted to show her that I was totally committed to her. So much so that I was willing to give her ALL of the game. She wanted to know, too. Men tend not to give women the game because it makes us look bad, especially when we tell our motivations behind why we do what we do. I took the risk of Nikki being totally repulsed when I told her why and how men dog women out. I was fearful that she would run in fear of me using the game on her. I let her know that even if she never chose me, at least she could recognize game when she saw it coming. At the end of the day, I just wanted what was best for her, even if that meant not being with me.

There is a street saying that states, "The game is meant to be sold, not told." You who are reading this book now, I sold you the game when I sold you this book. But to Nikki, I gave her the game free of charge. She was my sister and my best friend. I just had to, even if it made me look weak like a sucker.

After a lot of prayer and taking her out on dates, she finally came around and gave me a chance. She believed in me. We're still in love to this very day, otherwise I would have put another chick on the cover (ha ha). Nikki is truly the best thing that ever happened to me. She is good to me and for me.

Giving up the game can be a scary thing. The reason it's so scary is because many times when people think they have you figured out, the challenge is gone and sometimes people don't try as hard to be their best for you after a while. People will go out and give their boss at the job their best, they'll give their friends or Zumba class their best, but come home and treat their significant other like "chopped liver." The thrill and excitement of the chase is long gone and staleness sets in.

But it doesn't have to be that way, folks. Giving up the game, if you're so inclined to do so, isn't the end. You do have to go to work to keep it hot and exciting, though.

I was tired of the good-time girls who are only around when it's all new and exciting and the champagne is pouring. They are nowhere to be found when real life hits and you need them.

My wife may not be the sex-crazed chick you see in music videos gyrating and walking around in lingerie all the time, but she is as solid as they come. She's dependable, thoughtful and supportive. There's more ways to keep a man's attention than to dress skimpy. There are many women who know how to get or steal a man. They are "hot to death" and have their attraction and sex game on point. Ironically, with all of that, they are still single and don't know how to <u>keep</u> a man.

Hotties come a dime a dozen, but rarely know how to transition to wife status. We have a saying on the street, "You can't turn a whore into a housewife." This is true. I know it firsthand because I've tried it in times past. It brought me nothing but headaches and heartaches. But to know about what a keeper is like, read Proverbs Chapter 31 in the Holy Bible. Now that's game.

<u>NOTES</u>

CONCLUSION

With the knowledge you've gained so far, I believe now that your subconscious mind will recognize game coming from afar off. You'll have that inner tug to watch the actions of people and listen to the words they use with a more discerning eye and ear.

I want to drive home the point that the things I've revealed in this book were not meant to glorify my past lifestyle of manipulating women, nor am I advocating this type of behavior for any man or woman. If anything, I'm advocating saving sex for marriage, especially with all of the diseases and germs floating around in and through people these days. Also, with the numerous relationships before marriage, psychological damage is inevitable to say the least. I've used humor in this writing when expressing my experiences to drive home certain points, but there is nothing humorous when you are the one that has been hurt due to someone else's selfish unfaithfulness. I've been hurt and have hurt others. If this book can be a tool to prevent others from being used and abused, well then I would say it was all worth it.

GIVING UP THE GAME

Perhaps the best game is to not play them at all and simply be yourself. The purity in being exactly who God created you to be and knowing that he created you to love is the best gift you can give to yourself and to others.

RESOURCES

Weekend to Remember

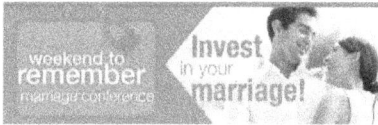

There's nothing in the world like weekend to remember. This helped our marriage tremendously. Weekend to Remember is a marriage conference held by Family Life all over the country. It is an excellent opportunity to invest in your marriage. Strengthen your relationship with your spouse as you listen to speakers on many marriage topics and have some time for the two of you to discuss and enjoy each other's company. Whether your marriage is good or struggling, this conference is amazing! If you go, you'll never regret or forget it.

Marriage Today

Marriage today has many resources to help married couples have happy fulfilling marriages. Since founding Marriage Today in 1994, Jimmy and Karen Evans have encouraged and coached countless couples in building rewarding marriages and healthy homes. With more than 50% of unions in America ending in divorce, the Evans are committed to sharing proven truths that can make the most troubled marriage good, and any good marriage great. Visit www.marriagetoday.com for more information.

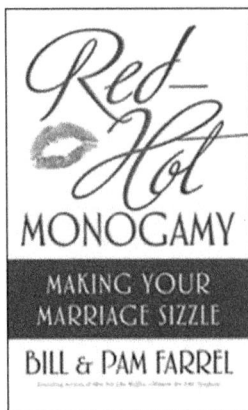

Red Hot Monogamy

With their trademark insight, humor, and candid personal perspectives, Bill and Pam Farrel reveal the truths about the sexual relationship in marriage and what husbands and wives need to know to keep the embers burning. This book should certainly help fan the flame of intimacy.

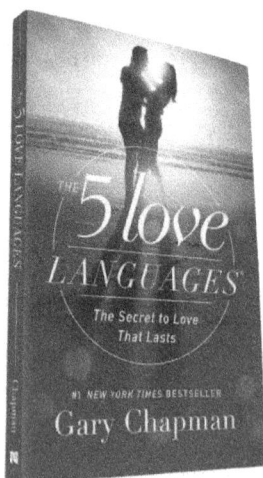

5 Love Languages

Between busy schedules and long days, expressing love can fall by the wayside. We forget to compliment, to give gifts "just because," to linger in our embrace. The things that say "I love you" seem to either not get said or not get through. This is a book about saying it—and hearing it—clearly. No gimmicks. No psychoanalyzing. Just learning to express love in your spouse's language.

With over **10 MILLION COPIES SOLD**, *The 5 Love Languages®* has transformed countless relationships. Its ideas are simple and conveyed with clarity and humor, making this book practical as it is personable. You'll be inspired by real-life stories and encouraged by its commonsense approach. Reading this book feels like taking a walk with a wise friend. Applying it will forever change your relationship—starting today.

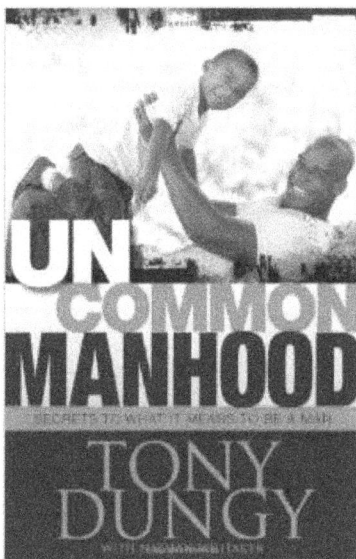

Uncommon Manhood

Too often we define a man's success by what he has rather than who he is. But Super Bowl-winning coach and bestselling author Tony Dungy knows that there's a better way. His deluxe gift book *Uncommon Manhood* will help you to celebrate the men in your life who have character, integrity, and courage. Men with both confidence and humility. Men who know the value of family and faith. Men who are truly uncommon. Adapted from Tony Dungy's *New York Times* bestseller *Uncommon*, this book is the perfect gift for dads, sports fans, young men, and anyone ready to embark on a life of uncommon significance.

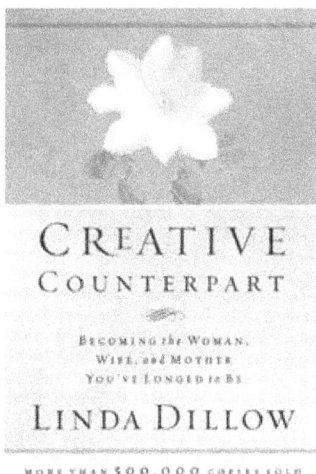

Creative Counterpart

Linda Dillow gracefully and succinctly motivates Christian women to reach for more than they are currently experiencing in their marriages. She includes creative suggestions on how to encourage your husband, live above your circumstances, and develop a plan whereby you can begin to become the woman, wife, and mother that you long to be.

A Healthier You

It's not only my home that you become healthier in your relationships, but healthier in body as well. The following company has the most amazing products that work. My family has benefited from our partnership with this company and I hope you will check them out and give them a try.

Go to www.treatyourbodyright.org TODAY!

THINKING   **HEALTH**   **RESOURCES**   **VILLAGE**

'Man Often Becomes What He Believes Himself To Be' ~Gandhi   'A Healthy Outside Starts from a Healthy Inside' ~Robert Urich   "Time and money spent in helping men to do more for themselves is far better than mere giving." ~Henry Ford   'Never doubt that a small group of thoughtful committed citizens can change the world.' ~Margaret Mead

"If You Help Enough People Get What They Want, then You Will Always Get What You Want." Zig Ziglar

Even if you eat right, exercise regularly, get plenty of sleep, and keep stress levels down, high quality supplements are still a critical part of fulfilling a healthy lifestyle.

OTHER WORKS BY THE AUTHOR

Transformed: The Past Doesn't Have To Define Your Future

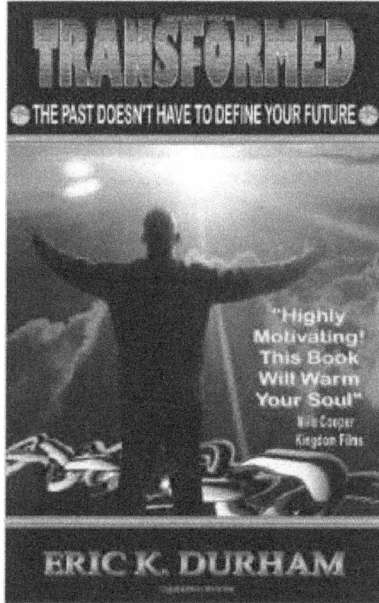

amazon.com

Customer Reviews

Dennis
Very Inspirational. Eric's book is captivating and incredibly inspirational. People of all ages can benefit from reading this awesome masterpiece.

Great lessons on the power of Faith, belief, desire, and the power of decision can be learned. This book can inspire and motivate the masses to make positive changes in their lives!

Carla
Great Read!! This is an AWESOME, life changing and transforming book. Definitely worth the investment. My teenage son also read it and it helped him also in his personal life.

Tanisha

Eric does such an amazing job on telling you the tale of his life. As a 20 year old from an urban area, I can relate to most of Eric's experiences and love how he explains his reflections through advice. I recommend to all especially those teens out there that need that push. Truly an inspiration.

Eric Durham: Florida's Con-fidence Man (DVD)

amazon.com

Customer Reviews

Mathias

Loved how this sleeper Doc show's how one man listened to Christ's voice and was determined to get out of the "CON-MAN" way of living and reach out to those considering following this crucial path. I realize watching this that this was done with minimal resources, but the message is here. We need more info about crime & the streets and how it's devouring our youth - at least for those who care anyway.

THE GAME HAS BEEN REVEALED...